I0764174

Cavalry Surgeon

Cavalry Surgeon

On Campaign Against Napoleon in the Peninsula & South of France During the Napoleonic Wars 1812-1814

S. D. Broughton

Cavalry Surgeon: on Campaign Against Napoleon in the Peninsula & South of France During the Napoleonic Wars 1812-1814
S. D. Broughton

Originally published under the title
Letters from Portugal, Spain & France 1812-1814

Published by Leonaur Ltd

ISBN: 978-1-84677-392-1 (hardcover)
ISBN: 978-1-84677-391-4 (softcover)

http://www.leonaur.com

Contents

Preface

The following account was were written originally at the request of a domestic circle of friends. The Author is aware that they possess very slender claims only to literary merit, and anticipates many objections that may be raised on the score of presumption, against his offering them to the Public, which would probably have greatly swayed with him in entirely suppressing them, if the lively interest recently taken in everything relating to the countries through which he passed, joined to the wishes, and perhaps partial commendation, of his friends, had not induced him to adopt an opposite resolution.

During the progress of a long march, commenced at Lisbon, and terminated at Boulogne, comprehending a tract of between fifteen hundred and two thousand miles, the Author made it his undeviating practice to note down faithfully, at the close of each day, every circumstance which appeared to him worthy of remark, and it was from these sources that he has been enabled to collect materials sufficient for the following series of Letters to his Friends.

Whatever may be its merits in other respects, it is at least entitled to that of unbiased veracity, as the Author has scrupulously abstained from recording any thing that did not immediately come within the sphere of his own observation, or upon the truth of which his own experience had not taught him to rely.

Throughout the Letters, the Author, from very obvious reasons, has studiously avoided giving any information, or expressing any opinion, upon military affairs, any farther than was necessary to give a general idea of events which it was desirable to notice slightly.

In conclusion, the Author feels it to be due to his own character to state that the speculations and prospective observations, which from time to time he has been disposed to indulge in, relative to the ultimate consequences of our successes in Spain, and the occupation of Paris by the Allied Armies, were written, it is well known, at a period long prior to the melancholy events which have since actually occurred.

Lisbon

Bellem, November, 1812. As soon as I had recovered from the fatigues of a very boisterous voyage, and surmounted the various difficulties attendant upon a first arrival in a strange country, and among people of habits and language so very different from those of our own, I recollected our mutual promise to correspond, and accordingly began a regular journal of events.

I commence my undertaking with the first opportunity that has occurred since our disembarkation, hoping to have closed it many hundred leagues hence; but, after the disappointments which have happened at Burgos, I much fear that for a long time I shall be under the necessity of confining my remarks to Portugal alone.

It is however to be wished, and probably to be expected, that the re-opening of the ensuing campaign will be more successful than the termination of the last, as our government must now feel convinced of the necessity of the greatest exertion, or of relinquishing the contest altogether. In the mean while as we shall no doubt towards head-quarters by slow degrees, I probably shall have many opportunities of becoming acquainted with the principal features of the country which we shall have to traverse.

Under the existing circumstances of the kingdom this is the most agreeable season of the year at Lisbon, when the breaking-up of the army and its getting into winter-quarters cause the town to be more frequented than during the spring or summer. It is accordingly now excessively crowded, not only with officers, but also with visitors, merchants, tradespeople &c. of all ranks and descriptions. Large meetings for society and amusement are held at Sir Charles Stewart's (the ambassador's), where a very handsome suite of rooms is open every alternate Monday, for dancing and cards, in addition to the occasional dinner-parties and more select evening assemblies; while the theatres, hotels, and gambling are all open and much resorted to.

The consul, Mr Jeffery, also gives very splendid balls and dinners, and some of the principal merchants follow his example; but the Port-admiral (Martin) does not entertain so much company as his predecessor, Admiral Berkeley. Water-parties up the Tagus and a few pleasant rides complete the principal sources of amusement. Upon all these I shall perhaps have occasion to remark in a subsequent letter, when I have had more time to pay attention to matters of this description.

Lisbon is so well-known that any minute description of it will be unnecessary; I cannot however refrain from endeavouring to give you an idea of the town and the adjacent country as they appear on entering the harbour, though it is difficult to do justice to the subject. On arriving, a short time before sun-set, in the broad mouth of the Tagus, the sudden contrast we experienced was extremely striking. We had quitted England in the worst autumnal weather, encountering the severest equinoctial gales, and suddenly we found ourselves transported to a mild and genial climate, very similar to that which we experience during the finest summer months in England. The sea was perfectly calm and the sky without a cloud, while the sun setting below the tops of the mountains cast a quiet shade upon their rocky surfaces, giving a delightful softness to the prospect, which, under a meridian sun, produces a sharpness of effect somewhat oppressive to an eye unaccustomed to southern latitudes. Upon our right rose the lofty and sombre hills of the Alentejo, and on our left the magnificent rock of Lisbon, towering at different points to an immense height, and stretching over a vast extent of country. Groves of olive and orange-trees interspersed upon its sides, contrasted with the grey granite of the rock, produced a beautiful effect. A few convents are built in these gloomy regions, and various religious houses crown even the loftiest summits of the mountains.

As we passed up the river, Cascaes, the Bugio Fort, Fort St. Julian, and Bellem with its castle projecting out towards the river upon the sands, Buenos Ayres, and Lisbon successively came in sight; the three latter exhibiting the appearance of one continued town which viewed at a distance from the extreme clearness of the atmosphere and the whiteness of the houses, produced altogether a splendor and brilliancy that was far from being realized on a nearer inspection; and the harbour, which is very spacious and convenient, being at this time crowded with ships, added much to the loveliness of the scene. Although I felt very desirous to quit the ship, and once more get a footing upon *terra firma,* yet recollecting that no foreign country affords that certainty of a comfortable reception to strangers which is so uniformly to be met with in an English inn, I thought it prudent to remain where I was for the night. The difficulties which I encountered the following day fully convinced me of the propriety of my resolution.

Hotels in all the three towns are to be met with, and by giving due notice a bad dinner, at a most extravagant price, may be procured; but at this time when the army was breaking up and reinforcements daily arriving from England, a bed was not easily to be found.

When I had cleared my baggage from the ship I had to encounter various perplexing difficulties in procuring a billet, which, after two fatiguing days spent in running about the town (before all parties concerned were accommodated) I at length effected, and obtained admission into an untenanted house (unless the rats, mice, and smaller race of vermin with which it swarmed can be regarded as inhabitants) possessing no other furniture than a few old chairs and tables, which however comprise all the domestic utensils absolutely indispensable to an officer's billet, when prepared for a campaign; his own bedding and canteen (which always accompany him) supplying every other deficiency.

I shall now close this letter in the expectation of being shortly able to give you some account of the principal objects worthy of attention in this city.

Lisbon II

*Bellem, November, 1812.*No sooner are we comfortably settled in our billets than we must turn our attention to provisions for a march, a circumstance which, from the instant of our setting foot upon dry land to the moment of our advance, should always have been considered as hanging over our heads "*in terrorem.*"

Accordingly I lost no time in going to the mule market, constantly held near the Roscio in Lisbon upon appointed days, unless any great saint's day or other church festival interfere. The demand being very great, and the venders monopolizing all the mules in the country for this market, cause the prices asked to be proportionably high: but as mules contribute so much to the comfort of officers while marching through desolated countries, it is adviseable to procure as many as you can persuade the commissary to feed. I have found these animals since my arrival peculiarly useful for riding, and probably shall in future become more sensible of their value in this point of view, as well as for the conveyance of baggage. They are generally very well broken in, quiet and docile, while their hardiness and sureness of foot render them better adapted than English horses for rough and common work. I have rode through the town upon one of them, and from the nature of most of the streets have reason to feel grateful to him for the preservation of my neck.

This excursion every where strongly reminded me of Sterne's exclamation on entering Paris;—"The streets, however, are nasty—but I suppose it looks better than it smells."

From the quantity and heterogeneous quality of the filth which is thrown from every window into the streets, without farther ceremony than sometimes a warning (which by law ought to be repeated thrice) of "*agua vai*," meant to caution the passengers that water is coming, you would naturally suppose that the people of Lisbon cannot be healthy in so hot a climate, constantly inhaling effluvia, the sources of which even the multitude of dogs (amounting, by a computation formerly made, to 80,000) that enter the town in the night is not sufficient to consume; and I assure you your supposition would be well founded, for the people in general appear very pallid and emaciated, arising, no doubt, from the above causes and their uncleanly mode of living.

The prevailing nuisance of throwing every species of filth into the streets is peculiarly striking to every one acquainted with the town as a most unpardonable negligence on the part of the police; a negligence the more extraordinary from Lisbon possessing so extensive and intimate an intercourse with England, and so many of the other European powers. When Junot occupied Lisbon, I understand he took the law into his own hands, ordered the streets to be cleansed, the filth to be conveyed to appointed reservoirs constructed for carrying it off into proper channels, and the hungry race of dogs—"their occupation gone"—to be destroyed. This gave equal offence to all parties concerned, and the abolition of the custom appears to have shocked public feeling as much as the existence of such a nuisance would in a town of our country. When the British power was resumed, this, among others of their good old customs and privileges, was restored. It is to be hoped, however, that time may effect improvements in the internal regulation of this great city, which policy alone, I conceive, has induced the British government to avoid attempting hitherto, and that when the work of reformation does begin it will be extended to other objects; for I suspect that the fullest account which has been given of the worst parts, and the most abandoned inhabitants of St. Giles's or the Borough, cannot exceed, perhaps not equal the depravity and squalid wretchedness prevailing in most parts of Lisbon.

But to turn to subjects of a different and more pleasing nature, I shall now proceed to give you a general description of the city itself. Ascending a very steep hill at the eastern end of the town you arrive at the castle, commanding a very fine and extensive prospect; but which, from its ruinous and imperfect state, has no other attraction. It was formerly a barrack, but is now a depôt for prisoners.

The houses of the Portuguese noblesse and rich merchants have an air of grandeur and splendor. But most of those forming the streets are in a very bad state of repair, though from their loftiness, balconies and whitened walls, they present an imposing appearance upon a cursory and general view. The streets are now better lighted than those of most English towns; though in former days they wanted this advantage, no lights being perceptible except some few faint glimmerings which superstition placed before statues of the Virgin Mary. It is consequently not so dangerous as formerly to walk through Lisbon at night, when robbers infesting the streets under the protection of darkness, and the contents of various vessels from the windows, united with the hungry dogs awaiting their fall, conspired to assail you with no trifling alarms. It is true the lamps are rather scantily distributed, but they are larger in size, and supplied with better oil than ours. Very few streets have any path-way raised upon their sides, which makes it disagreeable to foot-passengers. The two finest squares are the Roscio, and the Praca de Commercio. The former is more spacious, and less regular and handsome. The halls, offices &c. of the Inquisition formerly occupied a part of this square. The other square consists of lofty houses regularly and handsomely constructed, with piazzas to walk under, which take up three of the sides, the fourth being open to the river. In the centre stands a very fine equestrian Statue, in bronze, of one of the Josephs of Portugal. Two handsome streets also furnished with piazzas, called Gold and Silver-street connect the two squares, and form what may be called the Bond-street of Lisbon. There are also some public gardens (somewhat resembling those of Lincoln's-Inn) near the Roscio, in which the fashionables of the town occasionally walk. The arsenal is a tolerable building, but small and insignificant when compared with any structure of that nature in England. Horses are disembarked at this place, but (owing to the confined dimensions of the pier) only one ship at a time can be brought along side.

The churches particularly attract the eye of a stranger from their majestic size, and, in some instances from their elegance. The church dedicated to St. Paul in Buenos Ayres stands first in magnitude and beauty: it is composed of a kind of free-stone, which preserves its whiteness. The exterior is beautifully finished with carvings of scriptural histories, fret-work &c. It stands in a spacious open place railed round; and adjacent to it, and formerly connected with it, is a very magnificent convent now employed for hospital stores, and the offices &c. of the medical staff. The bridge which connects Lisbon with Bellem is a strong and handsome work, and is famous for a severe struggle when the French were driven away from the city. Bellem is a cleaner and pleasanter town to reside in than Lisbon. From the extremity of one to that of the other in includes a distance of about five or six miles. The prospect from the upper part of this town facing the entrance to the harbour is very fine, and from the neighbouring heights a cool and refreshing air is enjoyed. Bellem has always been the residence of the court. The Prince Regent has an old palace here in bad repair and dismantled of its furniture. The gardens are in somewhat better condition, and laid out in the same formal style which we see represented in the old prints of the gardens of the last century. They contain abundance of delightful orange-trees, at this season of the year creating the most fragrant scent, and loaded with fruit, with which those who visit the gardens are allowed to regale themselves. A botanic garden is attached to it, though not kept in the highest order. There is also a less pleasing though more curious novelty here in the form of an anatomical collection, where dry and wet preparations exhibit specimens of nature in most of her stages, together with numerous instances of *lusus naturæ*. Adjacent to the palace is a spacious and elegant riding school, where the royal stud is exercised and horses are broken in.

The manner in which the Portuguese break in their horses is somewhat curious, and has afforded me much amusement. These people appear to differ very decidedly from Englishmen in the ideas they entertain of the use which an horse should make of his legs. Weights are fixed to the animal's feet, which, in order to avoid entangling with his legs, renders it necessary for him to twist them in a very peculiar mode; and, when he has acquired the habit of going in this manner, with a sort of up-and-down motion having the appearance of moving with rapidity without any of the reality (very well calculated for the duties of parade), he is dismissed the school. The horses have their mouths rendered exceedingly tender, so as to require the lightest hand in exercising them to this singular kind of amble.

Upon the summit of the hill the Regent has a new palace in an unfinished state. It is built of a kind of white free-stone, or soft granite, and when completed will be one of the most magnificent buildings in Europe. But much yet to be done, and very little I believe, is in the royal coffers towards its completion. The ground and gardens surrounding the palace will be, when finished, very fine; but the park stands at a distance, and some little way from the town. It is well-walled round and wooded, and forms a delightful ride. Instead of being supplied with deer it is stocked with pigs of a small black kind living chiefly upon sweet acorns which gives their flesh a tenderness and delicacy of flavour unknown in our pork. I confess I should feel considerable alarm for their flavour if they should chance to make their escape from the park, and effect any alteration in their diet from the temptations they would encounter without the walls.

The next object which excites attention is the convent of Saint Jeronimo, and the church attached to it. These are very fine specimens of the gothic architecture. They are beautifully ornamented with carved work upon their porticos, arches &c. A few friars inhabit the former building, though the major part of it is assigned to the sick and wounded soldiers.

Upon the sands at the side of the harbour's mouth stands Bellem Castle, an ancient building with a tower, situated in a particularly strong position. There are gateways also indicative of fortifications formerly guarding this entrance to Bellem and Lisbon. I have now brought you to the end of a morning's tour, the account of which may be as fatiguing to you as the ride was to me.

Living in Portugal

Bellem, December, 1812. Having endeavoured in my last letter to give you a general idea of Lisbon as it appears upon a cursory view, I shall now proceed to give you some notion of the interior construction of the houses, and of the domestic arrangements of their inhabitants. The style of the old houses appears for the most part to be Saracenic, but that of the more modern ones seems to deviate occasionally from the ancient model; the more fashionable houses partaking somewhat of the refinement of Parisian elegance. In the oldest houses, dark, dirty and moth-eaten tapestry lines the walls, and covers the bedding and chairs. Almost every house is furnished with a balcony, it forming one of the chief amusements of the families to stand in it for hours looking into the streets. The panes of glass in the windows (always of a very inferior quality) are mostly broken to pieces, and are rarely as far as I can understand repaired; which indeed is the case with almost every thing in their houses. Their furniture seldom exceeds a few tables and chairs, and some grotesque figures of the Virgin and Our Saviour carefully preserved, with abundance of small crosses dispersed about the room: one of the latter is commonly suspended over a bason of holy water, and placed by the head of the bed in order (as they informed me) to defeat the machinations of evil spirits.

As the houses seem constructed entirely to alleviate the effects of heat, they are not calculated to reserve the inhabitants from cold, and, as a substitute for a grate, a small iron vase is used into which charcoal is put previously burnt to a red heat to dissipate the noxious fumes: but the unpleasant, and certainly unwholesome effect, which this mode of warming a room produces, frequently counterbalances the advantage derived from its heat. Wax being exceedingly dear, and tallow very indifferent, lamps are usually substituted for candles. The oil of the country is indeed very fine, and burns with a very bright flame. The table-lamps are usually made of brass, and are supported by a stem from one to two feet and an half high; but these are troublesome to manage, though when well trimmed they afford a very agreeable light. The natural indolence of the Portuguese occasions them to be careless and slovenly in their domestic arrangements. The dirt is rarely swept from the floors, and to the comforts of a scrubbing brush and soap and water they are total strangers. In order to dissipate the effluvia pretty generally prevailing in this town they are accustomed to burn dried lavender in all their rooms. With respect however to their house linen, I must do them the justice to say, they are more particular, having a great change which they never suffer to be long in use without being washed. Neither soap, nor any substitute for it, is used in this operation. Their mode of washing is performed by women, who are seen in groupes up to their knees in a running stream of water, and when they have rubbed, and squeezed, and dashed the linen sufficiently against large stones, it is spread around upon the banks to be dried and bleached by the sun, which soon gives it a beautiful whiteness. Ironing is used only among the higher circles for fine linen.

Observing the quantity of business perpetually going on in their kitchens, which with the use of the netting-needle and the distaff occupies the chief time of the females, you would suppose that the Portuguese lived well and kept good tables; the fact however, with the exception of the higher orders is the contrary, as they usually take very little food, and that not of the most nutritive quality; and it is so overdressed as to destroy the greater part of what little nourishment it may inherently possess.

Chocolate, rice, cabbage, oil, garlic, onions, pumpkins, chessnuts &c. form the basis of their principal dishes, into which animal food rarely enters, with the exception of *buccalao* or dried fish. Messes of these are constantly stewing over a little wood fire, and partaken of by every member of the family seated round the fire in the most patriarchal simplicity. But the more wealthy (though nevertheless not very agreeable to an English palate) produce an elegant assortment of dishes upon their tables, fine fruit, and pleasant light wines. The fault usually found with their cookery by Englishmen is the employment of too much art, and the very liberal distribution of garlic, oil, and onions throughout all their dishes.

The best produce of the markets consists of fresh and dried fruits; every other article, such as meat, fish &c. being scanty and inferior in quality. Among the vegetables the finest is a peculiar kind of onion remarkable for its great size and delicacy of flavour, and much prized by the English. It is difficult to preserve this sort of onion, though it finds its way to the English markets and is sold at a price bearing no comparison to what it fetches in this country where it is cheap and abundant. Chessnuts are sold in great quantities in the streets, which are roasted by women in little earthen furnaces constructed for this purpose and which they keep burning by the constant application of fans of wicker-work.

With respect to their carriages the following are chiefly in use. Cabriolets constructed to hold two persons and furnished with leathern fronts to be opened or shut at pleasure, and drawn by two mules, stand in the streets for hire. They are very rough, dirty, and slow machines; the driver, with a miserable cloak thrown over his shoulders, a large cocked hat upon his head, mounted upon an high wooden saddle, and his feet buried in large wooden stirrups, sitting upon the near horse. The better description of carriages consists of coaches and chariots curiously painted, and much resembling ours about two centuries ago; these are drawn by two, four, or six mules, according to the circumstances of the owner; the drivers being arrayed in tawdry and shabby liveries, with hats and stirrups, which, to those accustomed to the splendid decorations of a modern English carriage, beggars all description.

Whenever I pass through the streets I am constantly reminded of not merely being in a catholic town, but in one of peculiar bigotry and ignorance. People are seen kneeling and motionless before the numerous shrines which may be said to swarm throughout the whole city. Figures of the Virgin are preserved in glass cases, together with those of Christ upon the cross, and numberless collections of relics. These are hung against the walls of the streets, and are furnished with lamps upon particular occasions, as saints' days, festivals &c. The devout always uncover as they pass these emblems and it is common to see men going through the streets calling at every shop and house with figures of the Virgin (little dolls fantastically dressed), a kiss of which may be obtained for a *vintem,* a copper piece of about five farthings value. In like manner, at a particular sound of the church bell, when the host is elevated, they uncover, cross themselves, and strike their breasts. When the evening closes the lower orders are accustomed to place themselves at the thresholds of their doors to chant the rosary. Parties of the soldiery, recruits &c. are to be seen drawn up in lines performing this piece of devotion, and a curious kind of buzz is thus heard as you pass along, accompanied by an air of indifference among them which would lead one to doubt whether religion had any share in the ceremony.

You can seldom walk out without encountering the procession of the host with a priest going to perform the last offices of religion to some expiring penitent. The priest who administers the extreme unction walks under a canopy dressed in his robes, bare-headed, and with the holy wafer &c. in his hands, attended by a train of persons who assist in the ceremony carrying frankincense and the several religious utensils, preceeded by a man with a large bell to give public notice of the passing of the host. All persons as it goes along, whether within their houses or in the streets, kneel and cross themselves, and a large concourse of people usually brings up the rear of the procession chanting in unison with the priest.

While I am upon this subject I will relate two anecdotes that will serve to show the excess to which these people carry their devotion. The Marquis of——, an old Portuguese nobleman, passing full dressed in his carriage and during an hard shower of rain, encountered this sacred procession. Notwithstanding the inclemency of the weather he stopped his carriage, descended, and exposing his powdered head to the storm dropped upon one knee with the postillion in the street, and assuming his wonted dignity mounted again, and then drove on in full state to the place of his destination.

The other instance to which I allude occurred in the case of a poor woman, who, being ignorant of the host's passing by, emptied unwarily the contents of an earthern vessel from one of the highest windows of the house which fell upon the canopy borne over the priest. Discovering this sacrilegious ablution she uttered a scream, while her terrified hand let fall the vessel, and running down stairs sobbing and crying prostrated herself before the priest; who, in spite of the apparent heineousness of the offence, instantly absolved her from the guilt of this unintentional irreverence.

Such is still the awe in which the lower orders stand of the priests and the idolatrous faith with which they regard every thing that relates to priesthood and religious ceremony, that, I am credibly informed, the market-people and shop-keepers in general give a visible preference in the best choice of their articles exposed for sale to any priest who favours them with a visit, the honour of which is considered as sufficient payment. It is also supposed that by the presence of a priest, or that of a crucifix or image, the charms of all evil spirits are destroyed, no boat can sink upon the water, nor the witches effect their spells. We will now turn to the more imposing and respectable parts of the religion, which however time obliges me to defer till I can write to you again.

Religion

Bellem, Dec. 1812. I have been highly gratified and somewhat stonished from several visits I have been paying to the principal churches. The appearance of pomp, wealth, and splendor which they all exhibit in a greater or less degree, is calculated to have a striking effect upon those accustomed only to the more simple and modest discipline of the protestant church.

The most interesting church in Lisbon is that dedicated to St. Roque. The exterior of the building is heavy and without ornament; the interior contains a collection of church decorations the most valuable and magnificent in Portugal. Two large, massy, wrought silver gilt candlesticks, each ten feet high, stand before the principal altar. Junot robbed the church of these when he was driven from Lisbon, and took them to Almeida. They were afterwards brought back, and restored to their former situation by Lord Wellington's order. Candlesticks of silver gilt and less in dimensions, but beautifully worked, adorn the table of the altar, over which are suspended three large scriptural subjects in mosaic work. They appear upon a cursory view to be paintings of the first order in oil, but a closer inspection shows them to be composed entirely of small and beautifully coloured pieces of marble exquisitely arranged. Their value is inestimable, as you may imagine when you consider the enormous price which is paid for a small medallion only of mosaic work. Much magnificence is displayed throughout the whole assemblage of furniture in this altar. The curtains and hangings are of rich crimson velvet, ornamented with the finest broad gold embroidery, and lined with pale blue satin; richly gilded carving and fretwork forming the general relief. The communion-table consists of one uniform slab of *lapis-lazuli* with a deep border of gold, while its supporters and the different upright slabs and pillars around are formed of the most precious stones and marbles, such as *verde* antique, cornelion, porphyry, agate, alabaster &c. The floor and steps are composed of mosaic work. When I had sufficiently gazed upon all this magnificence my conductor took me to an obscure corner of the church, and opening a dirty wooden case shewed me a representation of the sacrifice of the lamb intended for an altar-piece; but its value being very great it had prudently been concealed during the residence of the French in Lisbon, and had never since been brought out. Its dimensions are nine feet by three. It is worked in solid silver, and gilt upon a ground of lapis lazuli. The figure of an angel about a foot and an half high, of silver gilt, supports the medallion in which the subject is worked on each side.

There are several other churches dedicated to various saints, differing in the degree of grandeur exhibited in their ornaments, though not materially in their general structure. They all produce, by the aid of crimson hangings and gaudiness, an imposing effect; which, together with the golden ornaments, paintings, images, carving and fret-work, artificial flowers, enormous candlesticks &c. form a very striking and grand appearance. Besides the great altars they have minor ones for particular days and occasions. Confessional boxes are also placed in different parts of the church, where a priest listens through a small grating to the penitential secrets of females confessing upon their knees. The patriarchal church at Bellem is very magnificent, and the service is performed with all the strictness of religious ceremony. The Prince Regent formerly attended this church, which being considered generally as the chapel royal is mostly frequented by people of the first fashion. Upon Christmas-eve it was lighted-up for the performance of grand mass, which lasted from about nine o'clock in the evening till two in the morning.—The splendor of the church was greatly increased by the lights, and produced a very brilliant effect. But the impression made upon my feelings was too theatrical, and I was more often reminded of a spectacle in Covent Garden than of a religious ceremony.

Imagine a spacious and lofty church adorned with gold carving and fret-work, paintings finely coloured, admirably executed and furnished with rich frames, magnificent long curtains of crimson velvet with deep gold embroidered borders; walls lined with hangings of the same description; rich carpets thrown over the steps of the altar, the floor covered with baize:—the splendor of the whole heightened by brilliant lustres, while the grand altar itself formed one blaze of light, and a pyramid of the brightest colours from the mixture of artificial flowers, brilliants, ribbons, silks, satin and gold work, altogether exhibiting a scene of gorgeous magnificence to which no description can do justice; and you will probably have some idea of the sensations I experienced at such an exhibition. The bottom of the chancel is separated from the body of the church by very elegant gates of curiously wrought lion-work with gold ornaments. These were thrown open to give the concourse of people who thronged the church a view of the ceremony; but beyond this limit they were not allowed to pass, with the exception of British officers, and some other strangers who were permitted to stand right and left of the altar. The former were principally upon their knees during the ceremony, and preserved a profound silence. A number of persons of fashion of both sexes attended, dressed in their most superb attire. On the right of the altar, towards the bottom of the chancel, the canons of the church were ranged in the full parapharnalia of cardinals, with each his train-bearer at his feet. Opposite to these sat the bishops. At the front of the altar a chair of white satin, embroidered with gold, was placed for the patriarch, who officiates at this church as the Pope's representative dressed in every respect like his holiness on similar occasions. He was a mild and venerable looking old man, with a feeble voice, though impressive manner. He was supported and assisted in the ceremony by a numerous train of clergy, and a number of the lower orders of ecclesiastical attendants, whose formal entré and exit at different parts of the service reminded me rather too forcibly of a premeditated exhibition. The music, which seldom ceased during the rites, was solemn and affecting. The orchestra is furnished with a very superior organ, which, together with a band of Italian singers, produced the finest choruses I ever heard. The band contained at this time several first-rate vocal performers who executed beautiful duets, solos &c. one of them being reckoned the finest singer in Europe, and esteemed equal to Madam Catalani. I have before remarked that the whole of these ceremonies in the eyes of those of a different persuasion wears too much the appearance of affectation and mummery; but, if it be ever possible to abstract the mind from feelings of this nature, it is during the consecration of the wafer, and the elevation of the host. Then, as Gibbon says, "I felt myself a catholic." On a sudden the music ceases—the profoundest silence reigns throughout the church, and every individual is upon his knees—the patriarch prays in silence— a deep and hollow toned bell on the top of the church (by a signal from below) sounds twice or thrice at short intervals—the people cross themselves, strike their breasts, and bow their heads to the ground—a pause ensues—the patriarch, with his eyes lifted to heaven, rises, and elevates the consecrated wafer—a beautiful swell of the full organ, accompanied by a chorus, instantly bursts forth, producing the grandest and most awful effect.—This formed the conclusion of the ceremony, and I left the church, with feelings which no language is adequate to describe. The following day one of the singers conducted me round the church, and through the various rooms adjoining, when I was surprised to find that all the large and glittering stones of the mitre and other parts of the costume were false; the French having taken away the real jewels, of which, however, these were said to be exact imitations. Great quantities of lace, the finest linen, silks, and gold embroidery were likewise at the same time pillaged to an immense amount: some part of these valuables, however, escaped the cupidity of the spoilers, many of which still remain. The finest church collection of paintings in the city is said to belong to this establishment. Several of the best are kept in private; though Junot, according to his usual practice, carried off many specimens of the art.

In one of the anti-rooms they exhibit a curious model representing the creation, in which almost every possible thing and being is imitated. The convent and church dedicated to Saint Jeronimo are very fine specimens of ancient architecture. The former is now appropriated to sick and wounded soldiers, a few apartments being still inhabited by some friars: a great variety of single figures and scriptural histories beautifully carved ornament the porticos.

At this season of the year a stage built before one of the altars displays the Nativity in figures larger than life, and literally agreeing with the whole description of the situation in which Our Saviour was found at his birth. During this representation a plate is placed upon the stage to receive donations for the convent.—On the night of Christmas-eve the ceremony of the different circumstances of the Nativity is performed.

I have occasionally been present at some requiems, and other musical festivals. These are calculated to fill the mind with feelings very different from those inspired by the mere mummery of mass, and superstitious processions; the effect produced by their harmony I shall never forget; it was really sublime; and however much I may prefer in a devotional point of view the mild simplicity of the religious discipline of the church of England, yet it appears to me no way surprising that an immense mass of the people should continue pertinaciously attached to the imposing ceremonials of the catholic religion. Ignorant and unenlightened as they are, how can they be otherwise affected? when power, pomp, and mystery surround the officers, and accompany the practice of religion, while the eye is dazzled with magnificence, and the ear delighted with the finest music. The ancient power and respectability of the Romish church has been, however, rapidly declining in Portugal; the removal of the Inquisition by the French having opened the eyes of the inhabitants, and taught them to think with more freedom and liberality than before. A long continued connexion with England will no doubt render catholicism still milder and more inoffensive, and probably lessen the ignorance and bigotry yet existing.

The clergy, upon their part, having got rid of the tyranny exercised by the French, it may be readily supposed want no inclination to restore their power and consequence in the eyes of the people, and the influence they held over their minds. But this there is little chance under existing circumstances of their bringing about to any considerable extent, though possibly among the least enlightened they may effect their purposes partially. Such was the terror, during the residence of the French in Portugal, which all religious orders felt in being recognised, that they suffered their tonsures to be obliterated, in order to avoid this characteristic mark of their profession; and such were the persecutions they sustained, that whatever may be our opinions respecting the policy of priestcraft, so much cherished by the Catholic religion, yet the tales of woe related concerning these unfortunate men must excite pity and commiseration even among those who hold their principles in the utmost abhorrence. They have now, however, resumed their tonsures and their accustomed clerical habits, and with these some degree of respect is regained among the people, though not in the degree commensurate with their ambitious views.

In the present day it is no unusual thing to meet with many Portuguese who will descant upon these subjects with a degree of freedom, which .a few years past would inevitably have exposed them to the severest chastisement of the Inquisition. An intelligent and respectable officer of artillery in the company of a party of British and Portuguese officers, who (like Mr. Shandy,) "hated a monk, and the very smell of a monk, worse than all the devils in hell," declared it to be his firm belief that all the misfortunes of his country were to be attributed to the prevailing system among the nobles and gentry of the land of breeding up their sons to the church, and under the direction of the priests, instead of introducing them to the secular duties of the state; by which means a large proportion of the most important part of the community had their minds contracted, and were subjected to the influence of bigotry and superstition. He added (in a satyrical tone) so offensive to his feelings was the sight of a monk that he never encountered one without considering it as an ill omen, and that some misfortune would happen to him during the day on which so unlucky a meeting had occurred.

Wellington

Bellem, Jan. 1813. The instances which I gave you in the former part of my last letter of devotion and respect for religion would naturally lead to a supposition that Sunday must be observed with a more profound reverence and abstinence from worldly pleasures and pursuits, than is customary in protestant countries. The fact, however, is quite the reverse. Pleasure and religion go hand in hand, and the followers of both worship either with equal ardor. In the morning the churches are scarcely more crowded than the theatres in the evening. When the bells have ceased ringing for mass the guitars give the sign for fandangos, boleros, and waltzing. Labour, Indeed, of every description is at a stand, but it is merely to give a fuller nope to all sorts of recreation. Sunday is the gayest day of the week; the prados are more crowded, and pleasure of all descriptions becomes the order of the day.

The theatres in Lisbon are in general very indifferent, and scarcely worthy of notice; I shall therefore confine myself to the principal one called "*Teatro de San Carlos*," which is open every night in the week. Operas, comedies, farces, ballets, and dancing, are all performed here alternately. It is a large, gloomy, and very badly lighted house, somewhat in the form of our Opera-house, but not so large, and without any pretensions to vie with it in elegance or beauty. The boxes are ranged like ours, with the exception of the royal box, which is spacious, lofty, and placed in the centre of the circle. There is no gallery, but a very large and commodious pit and an extensive orchestra. The stage is very spacious, and tolerably lighted, but the scenery is ill painted, and very indifferently managed. At one period perhaps this opera was unrivalled in Europe; during the time that the court resided in Lisbon, and Junot was ambassador from the French court, when Catalani and several of the first singers were engaged, and the elder and the younger Vestris, and Angiolini were the principal supporters of the ballets. The Portuguese ladies usually adopting black for their full dress, and the gentlemen not being very gay in their costume, gives a sombre appearance to the boxes, when contrasted with the gay and lively exhibition which a well-filled row of boxes presents in an English theatre. Sentries are placed at different points in the pit and lobbies, who control every expression of approbation or discontent in the audience that affords the slightest interruption to what is going forward. The lobbies are furnished with a refectory, where lemonade, punch, liqueurs, coffee and cakes are plentifully supplied. They have also, as the Portuguese are very fond of gambling, a lottery always open, where you pay a trifle for a handful of twisted little pieces of paper, which, after much time spent in unravelling, produce either a blank, or some trumpery prize not worth carrying away; but such is the passion for this mode of amusing themselves among the Portuguese, that hundreds will spend their time in the lottery-room, in this manner. Above stairs are gambling-tables of an higher description. These kind of places are well known in the army by the very appropriate term of hell, and I am sorry to say that I have witnessed here many a painful scene. You would scarcely be induced perhaps to believe that the desire of winning money is by no means in every instance the chief stimulus to play. The following anecdote will show that the practice of the vice of gambling is sometimes more a matter of habit than an innate love of gain. A *fidalgo* in Lisbon (well known for his dwarfish appearance,) though he had no money to risk himself, was always so eager to play, that he was in the habit of begging of one of the company to lend him a doubloon, with which he sat down. If he was successful he gave the person from whom he borrowed the money all his winnings, accompanied with the warmest thanks; and as our little nobleman was one of the most expert amateurs in gambling, it was deemed no bad speculation to lend him money in this manner, by those who were less confident of their own proficiency, and had no objections to add to the little they might have to venture. Besides San Carlos there is a tolerable little theatre at Bellem, called the *"Boa Horn,"* where operas, comedies, farces &c. are performed. I have usually recognized in the comedies and farces of the Portuguese either complete translations or partial imitations from our comic muse. It must be confessed that there is no great occasion for jealousy on our parts; for when witticisms, only supportable from accidental and local circumstances of the passing day, are literally copied upon the Portuguese stage, you may readily conceive the brilliancy of their effect.

Next to the theatres the different hotels are the chief places of public resort, provided those who prefer them have no regard to œconomy or comfort, neither of which in these places is to be expected. The most execrable of all are one or two kept by Englishmen, who go beyond even the Portuguese in extortion. One of the most celebrated hotels is that of Monsieur La Tour, which commands a fine prospect of the river and the sea. But its various internal disadvantages so completely counterbalance its exterior beauties, that I have been rarely tempted by the persuasive and irresistible witticism, which the host has indulged himself in by placing (in the room of his name, as a pun upon it,) a large gilt Tower over the door. The many accidents however to which you are exposed in ascending the stairs would probably deter the most curious inquirer from any further research.

During three days the town has lately been rendered very gay by the presence of Lord Wellington. His arrival had been anxiously looked for some time previously, as he had not been in Lisbon since the period of its complete liberation from the French yoke. The preparations for his reception were extensive and grand. He arrived from Cadiz at a small place in the Alentejo, about nine miles across the Tagus, and landed in Lisbon on the following day. The weather was very fine, adding considerably to the general festivity of the day. A large boat belonging to the Regent, splendidly decorated, was rowed across, to bring him and his staff to the steps of the great commercial square. Every ship in the harbour was dressed, and the part of the river was covered with boats of all descriptions, gaily trimmed and adorned. The windows, balconies, and tops of the houses were filled with well-dressed people, and the streets below were crowded to excess. The Life-Guards kept the ground from the landing steps, which they fruitlessly endeavoured to guard from the interruptions of the populace, while the British and Portuguese infantry, with their bands and colours, formed a lane to the palace of the Necessidades, where Lord Wellington was to take up his residence. He was received at the landing-place by a very brilliant assemblage in full dress, consisting of the British Ambassador, (Sir Charles Stewart), the Members of the Regency, Marshal Beresford, and a concourse of British and Portuguese officers of all ranks and distinctions; some of the Prince's led horses and state carriages were in attendance, the former richly caparisoned, and the servants in their state liveries. About half-past two a salute from the flag-ship announced his Lordship's approach, which was the signal for the commencement of a scene of grotesque and tumultuous joy rarely paralled: cheering and firing from the shipping, shouts of "*viva*" from the Portuguese, varieties of bands playing as many different tunes as there were instruments, squibs, crackers, and all kinds of fire-works, with horses, mules and donkies prancing and braying in all directions, ushered the hero upon shore. Immediately as the Marquis stepped out of the boat the populace, maddening with joy, burst through all obstructions, and rushed upon him with one accord in an overwhelming torrent. Among them an old priest actually clung to him, and could with great difficulty be pulled away, calling him the preserver and saviour of the country, the deliverer of the church &c. As soon as he could disentangle himself from these friendly hugs and caresses he mounted his horse, dressed in a plain gray frock coat, with his generals and all the other great people glittering with stars and orders. Having passed round the line of the household troops, he proceeded to the palace of the Necessidades, attended by an escort of one of the regiments of Life-Guards.

In this scene of national exultation it may be supposed that the ladies took no inconsiderable share, expressing their joy by waving their white handkerchiefs in the air and casting flowers upon the head of their adored champion, as he passed under their windows.

I had never seen this great man before, but in a very casual way, and was much struck with his appearance. There is an animation and intelligence in his countenance, which, joined to the native dignity and simplicity of his deportment, was remarkably interesting and impressive.

During the three days he remained in Lisbon every mark of esteem and honor was shewn to him. The city and the armed vessels in the harbour were illuminated every night, as were even the convents and churches; a mode of rejoicing from which, as they formed the most splendid part of the exhibition, a beautiful effect was produced. Generally speaking, however, the illuminations in this country are very inferior to those which are common in England.

The evening after the Marquis's arrival (Sunday,) the opera-house presented a scene of novelty and magnificence to which the audience had been unaccustomed, the house being then more splendidly lighted up and adorned than usual, and the performances of a superior kind. Lord Wellington, with some of his friends and the Members of the Regency, sat in the Regent's box, and most of the general officers and staff were superbly dressed in boxes upon his right and left.

Upon this occasion no ordinary exertions were made on the part of the citizens in general to prove the devoted and enthusiastic admiration in which they held (as they termed him) "*Nosso Grande Lorde.*" All the talents of Lisbon united to get up a piece suitable to the event. The opera represented, or at least was intended to represent, the Elysian Fields, in which all the Portuguese heroes of antiquity (exclusively) were seen to enjoy themselves. Fame descended amongst them, and proclaimed the glorious deeds of *Velington,* which the goddess (without any regard to the feelings of the heroes around her) declared to eclipse all others that were ever recorded, coupling with this declaration every epithet of love and adoration which a Portuguese imagination could conjure up. The departed spirits, (jealous of this assumption of superiority) entered into a warm dispute with Fame upon the subject; she, however, remained perfectly obdurate, while they, on their parts, did not appear the least inclined to resign the palm. Fame then boldly told them that none of them had done any thing which could bear a comparison with the deeds of the "*Grande Lorde.*" Upon this the Marquis de Pombal (their favourite hero and one of the principal figures in the group,) came forward with looks of astonishment at Fame's presumption, and exclaimed—"What! did *I* do nothing?" to which the deity, with evident anger at her authority being doubted, replied— "No, not even *you!*" and thus put an end to the dispute, upon which the audience testified their unanimous approbation, without the least regard to the honor of their countrymen. It was intended to commence the spectacle by causing a crown of laurel to descend upon Lord Wellington's head as he entered the box; but, lest by accident, their good wishes should be perverted, and something ludicrous produced by its falling on the wrong head, his Lordship declined this honor.

On the Monday night following, Sir Charles Stewart gave a very splendid ball and supper to all the principal people in Lisbon, including a great portion of the officers in the town, but no one was admitted without a ticket, (which on ordinary nights is not required,) in order to limit the company at the supper tables. The entertainment was very sumptuous, and the whole well arranged. The ambassador's residence is very spacious and handsome, and was built by a rich merchant for his own accommodation. At the assemblies held here you meet with all the fashionable society, which, after the emigration of the court, was left in Lisbon.

Their manners, customs, and style of dress are very different to those of the polished classes of our own country. The ladies both in person and manners are certainly inferior to our own, though there is nothing peculiarly offensive in their conduct and appearance: a roundish plump face, rather sallow complexion, with more or less colour, and lively hazle eyes, with long black eye-lashes, and dark hair, appear to form the general character of their countenances, some of which are very interesting and pretty. They generally wear black, when dressed, intermixed with a little white; their waists short; and when they walk out, a long laced mantle is thrown over the head, which they hold with one hand under the chin, while the other is constantly employed in carrying a fan. Excepting at evening assemblies, in the theatres, and on their way to mass, the ladies are seldom or ever seen in public. Upon the latter occasion their duennas usually follow them, and their deportment is then grave, somewhat solemn and dignified. Upon other occasions they exhibit a degree of gaiety and vivacity which in the eyes of a stranger rather borders upon levity; and, you may rely upon it, that the character and disposition of the Portuguese ladies is in reality no means reserved and sedate. They are in private society inclined to be open and unreserved, often coquetish, and not inaccessible to flattery. They are not however to be taken by storm, but require a long siege, which, if the lover has patience to go through all the manoeuvres of it, is I believe rarely unattended with ultimate success. This I conceive does not arise from any previous intention and disposition to refuse advances altogether, but rather, I believe, from a not uncommon inclination to increase by delay the pleasure derived from tormenting the besieger, and the gratification attendant upon a prolonged address. Whether this casual description of the Portuguese ladies differs much from that of the ladies of other countries of Europe I leave you to judge; but you must not forget that the national feeling is now strong and powerful in our favour, and that the general enthusiasm may well be supposed to have increased the natural warmth and kindness of the softer sex.

Dancing forms one of the principal amusements in all their parties. Their balls usually commence with country-dances, succeeded by waltzing, which is commonly kept up till the party separates. The Portuguese waltz faster than the Germans, and more in the French style.

I have been to some private parties, the society of which gives you a more favourable idea of the Portuguese than you would at first be impressed with. Many of the gentlemen imitate the English costume, throwing off the enormous cocked hat, and dingy brown or black cloak in which the generality envelope themselves.

I cannot say that I have met frequently with much learning and information among them, though a few individuals possess considerable intelligence: but much cannot be expected where education is so little attended to.

There is somewhat of elegance and taste occasionally displayed in the better kind of houses, but no attention is paid to comfort, and still less to cleanliness in their general domestic arrangements.

The men are universally addicted to smoking segars, while the women appear to have an equal predeliction for garlic, and the disgusting habit of spitting, often without regard to time or place.

In my occasional intercourse with Portuguese society I have usually found something peculiar to arrest my attention; a ludicrous instance or two of which I will give you as specimens; one, the most distinguished compliment that a Portuguese can pay to a lady, by way of a salutation is—"*Adeosina, cada vez mais linda, mais alta, mais nova, mais blanca, et mais gourda:*"— "Good morning, Madam, you appear every time handsomer, taller, younger, fairer, and fatter:" and the other that, as it is considered no small indication of wealth and importance, and consequently a great compliment to notice it, if any one possesses a rotundity of person, such being considered a marked trait of a *'Fidalgo;'* he is described as a perfect nobleman in his appearance, and to feed on 'buccalao,' (salt fish,) beans, white bread, and plenty of oil with his herbs, luxuries not so much enjoyed by the vulgar. With these observations I shall conclude my remarks upon the capital, and here finish my letter.

Outside Lisbon

Lisbon, February, 1813. Since I dispatched my last letter I have made some excursions to neighbouring places, and I have just time sufficient before our removal from Lisbon to give you a short account of the most interesting features of my tour.

About six miles from Lisbon the Prince Regent has a palace in the village of Queluz, which formed his country residence. The road leading to it is nearly straight, well paved, and lies for the most part over stoney hills. It is a neat and agreeable place, surrounded by forests and pasture land. The latter part of the road from Lisbon is lined on each side with myrtles and geraniums, growing wild and in great perfection, the perfume of which extends to a considerable distance around, forming a striking novelty to those who have only been accustomed to more northern climates. The palace is a large and very handsome building, and the rooms are spacious and numerous. It is built with red brick, and was fitted up and adorned principally by the French, and completely in the Parisian style; the Regent at his departure for the Braziles having taken with him all the more valuable and moveable part of the furniture. The paintings upon the ceilings and walls are by the first artists. The couches, chairs &c. are light, costly, and elegant. The grand hall of audience is lined with large mirrors, and the pillars round the room are ornamented in a similar manner. The carving of all the rooms is generally well done, and that of the banqueting-room is peculiarly rich and excellent, but, the palace in general is out of repair. Great preparations were made here for the reception of Buonaparte, who however from the un-looked-for turn of affairs disappointed public expectation.

In one of the rooms of an octagon shape I observed the history of Don Quixotte beautifully painted, and many very fine portraits and landscapes by the first masters were interspersed throughout the other apartments.

The gardens are agreeably laid out, though not perhaps in the very best taste. They are decorated with a variety of very handsome bridges, temples, water falls, fish-ponds &c. The park, woods, and pleasure-grounds are extensive, and afford ample scope for the diversion of sportsmen, abounding with wild boars and game of many kinds. It is a singular circumstance that the dignified clergy possess the right of shooting in these, as well as (I believe) in every other royal park in the kingdom, and have the additional advantage of extending this privilege to other persons.

About fourteen miles from Lisbon, towards the sea, lies the town of Cintra, which will ever be in the remembrance of Englishmen, on account of the celebrated convention bearing its name. The road from Lisbon to this place is very rough and stony.

In order to view the beauties of the surrounding country we found it necessary to quit our horses, and to hire mules and donkies, which from their sureness of foot are better calculated for surmounting the steep precipices and various difficulties with which the neighbourhood abounds.

Imagination cannot, I think, conceive the sublimity of the scene from the heights, which include a most extensive prospect both by sea and land.

Shakespear's Cliff is a mere mole-hill to them. The rock of Lisbon, formed by a chain of stony mountains, reaches to these parts, and produces a most beautiful and striking effect. From this mountainous part of the country all the lower towns and villages are supplied with water by the different aqueducts, and the numerous plantations around are also irrigated by fruitful streams issuing from the rocks.

The principal aqueduct is highly deserving of attention as a magnificent and elegant work. Close to the suburbs of Lisbon, after emerging from the mountains, it is thrown across a broad valley by lofty and beautiful arches composed of an handsome granite, and soon after again enters the earth, and deposits its stream into several finely-worked and spacious reservoirs, furnished with delightful fountains; thus drawing water from rocks and mountains many leagues distant from Lisbon, and presenting a stupendous work worthy even of the genius of the Romans. This noble aqueduct was built in the reign of John V. during the early part of the last century. This monarch appears to have been one of the most public spirited that ever reigned in Portugal, many other remarkable works being indebted to him for their origin.

After we had satiated ourselves with the delightful scenery around us we returned to our inn, where a more substantial species of gratification awaited us in the shape of an excellent dinner dressed in the English style, for which however we paid pretty dearly; a circumstance very usual when, as in this case, the inn was kept by a British subject.

Following the example of others, before we quitted these parts we went on a little farther, in order to see the grand and extensive convent of Mafra, built by the same patriotic monarch who erected the great aqueduct; and who also endowed this sumptuous monastery with a valuable library. The convent of Mafra contains a royal palace beneath its roof; and thus, by the union of ministers both of church and state, seems lo have been intended to bring closer under the influence of the monks the bigotted sovereigns of Portugal. The length of the building in front is very considerable, and possesses an air of combined simplicity and grandeur in an high degree; very few I believe in Europe exceed it in size. The approach to it is fine, and you ascend a grand fight of steps to the entrance. A beautiful chapel, furnished with a good toned organ, forms a striking portion of the building. The monks had great influence over the present Regent, who is not, even by his own countrymen, famed for any of the higher virtues and qualities of the mind. During the invasion of the kingdom by Junot in 1807 (I believe,) at the time the enemy was almost at the gates of Lisbon, these devout men had complete possession of his Royal Highness's mind, and kept him employed in chanting and prayer whilst the roar of French cannon was announcing the captivity of his subjects. Without the interference of England the conquest of Portugal by France no doubt would have been but the work of a day. Junot, like Cæsar, might have said—"*Veni, vidi, vici*" But, when the incubus of a miserable priest-ridden government was removed, the Portuguese became more respectable at home, and more formidable (as we have seen from their fine army,) to their enemies.

Having touched upon such subjects as I thought might interest you regarding the neighbourhood of the capital, I shall now conclude. Probably my next letter will be dated some distance hence.

The Lines at Torres Vedras

Chamusca, February, 1813. Since writing my last letter we have moved from Bellem towards the headquarters of the army; and I must say I felt no small gratification in gelling clear of the dirt and effluvia of Lisbon, and once more enjoying a purer air together with the novelties incident to a march in this country, which during the delightful weather we have experienced is far preferable to the dull monotony attendant on a long residence in one place. Very few objects worthy of observation lay in our route. The country in general is fertile, finely variegated and pleasing. Olive and orange-groves flourish in abundance, and in this neighbourhood are found very fine and extensive vineyards, yielding wine which is of the best quality, and retailed at about four-pence a bottle.

In every town and village we have passed through the effects of the unprincipled conduct of the French army are conspicuous, which has Maturely caused their name to be held in utter abhorrence; and yet their barbarities are much less severely felt than I understand them to have been in more remote parts. A small portion of retail trade is carried on in most of the places through which we have passed, and in this neighbourhood in particular large quantities of wine are exported. The land also is daily improving in cultivation, though the arts of agriculture are at a comparatively low ebb. About six leagues from Lisbon on the left my attention was of course attracted by a part of Lord Wellington's extensive lines coming in view; of which, as they constitute a very prominent feature in the history of the campaign, I shall endeavour to give you some idea; particularly as I have obtained my information upon the subject from authority on which I can most fully rely. After Lord Wellington had fought the battle of Talavera, the result of which was unquestionably in our favour, he was obliged, from circumstances which it will be unnecessary to enumerate in this place, to relinquish his position, in consequence of Soult's bold and unexpected movement upon Placentia in conjunction with Mortier.

The country upon which he was forced to retire was unfortunately of the worst description and after a sickly sojourn in Estramadura, ever the grave of armies tarrying there, his Lordship fell farther back, and finally retreated to Portugal. This retreat, so bitterly lamented by the allied countries, and by England in particular, again roused the desponding bodings of opposition; and the firm belief in the never-failing ascendancy of the French arms, together with the idea of the almost absolute insanity attendant upon our endeavours to put a stop to their progress:—but the vigour of the masterly mind which directed these operations was only increased by the doubts thus cast upon its great military capacity.—His Lordship was aware of the tremendous means that could be employed to force the British army from the Continent; and he was equally convinced that the enemy would put every resource in motion to accomplish this great object, well knowing that this important point once obtained, all minor difficulties would vanish.

To this end he resolved on that plan of warfare that eventually proved the key-stone to his own glory and the deliverance of Europe. In 1809 he determined upon fortifying a position, which being unassailable in its flanks, would render the great superiority of the enemy's numbers of little avail; and by being far within the country would tend to draw the enemy rapidly to the extremity of the kingdom, where of course he could have no magazines, and where every resource might be cut off even by the inhabitants themselves; so that his difficulties would be multiplied, his destruction rendered more probable, and the safety of the allied army provided for. The position selected by his Lordship for the attainment of these great ends was one which covers Lisbon at a distance of more than six leagues from the city, defending every road to the capital through the great province of Beira, the very centre and heart of the kingdom, and which upon the best military opinions must always form the great object of attack. This celebrated position had its right resting upon the Tagus at Alhanda, whence it stretched across to Porte de Roll on the sea, and had consequently the most powerful apuis for both flanks, whilst its rear remained open and clear to all sorts of supplies. The position which I am now hastily describing, and which in 1810 occupied so important a point in the attention of Europe, was formed by a chain of hills running in the direction already mentioned; the most commanding of which, and particularly those principally overlooking the approaches to the capital, were occupied by strong redoubts, that on the advance of Massena were garrisoned principally by the Portuguese troops; the infantry (chiefly British) were judiciously posted in the long intervening spaces, to oppose the enemy should he attempt to penetrate, forming a chain of curtains to the redoubts.

The grand redoubt of the position occupied the rear of Sobral; and Torres Vedras also came within the line. This principal redoubt was occupied by 1500 men, and thither Lord Wellington came every morning, and thence could reconnoitre almost his entire position. The whole of this extensive line was not occupied: it was unnecessary that it should be so; for the direction in which the great Estrella mountains run through Beira, cutting that part of the kingdom in two, made it impossible for the enemy in front of the position to make any considerable movement to either flank, in half the time that the army in the position could make a corresponding one. There was also, in addition, a second line taken up and occupied much in the same manner, furnished with redoubts that ran through Bucillas, Mafra &c. *&c.* &c. and military encampments were made near St. Julian, which would have assisted embarkation, in case of any unforeseen disaster occurring in front that might have called for such a measure. A strong position in like manner was fortified on the left bank of the Tagus, in order to ensure the safety of the ships in the river in the event of the enemy moving in force on that side; and the whole military resources of the river being at Lord Wellington's disposal, the enemy could never have reached the capital from that quarter. The influence of the British general over the Portuguese nation was paramount, for he was to all practical purposes King of Portugal; and Sir Charles Stewart, our Envoy, having also a seat in the government, there was less difficulty in carrying into effect any arrangements in contemplation. The removing the supplies of the country out of the enemy's reach, thereby rendering the land through which he was to pass a waste, was part of this extensive plan; though much difficulty occurred in carrying this portion of it into execution; for the Portuguese government could hardly be induced to accede to any measure that would bring so powerful and dreaded an enemy close to their very gates. The firmness however of Lord Wellington prevailed; and it was, I am told, an heart-rending spectacle to see the poor inhabitants turning out of their dwellings with their children and moveables, flying in all directions—to misery and death, the cavalry was stationed in the rear, and upon the left flanks, in which latter situation they were a great annoyance to the enemy, who was obliged to forage extensively. Generals Silviera and Trant were posted in the north, and consequently during the enemy's sojourn before our position operated successfully upon his rear.

Such were the preparations for the great campaign of 1810, which in immediate consequences overthrew one of the enemy's most powerful armies, and liberated the kingdom of Portugal. In its more remote consequences it held out a cheering example to the nations of Europe, and eventually animated them to successful resistance; a campaign which completely falsified the predictions of those who prophecied the most disastrous results, and in its sequel exceeded the most sanguine expectations; a campaign which by the fair operation of superior tactics, and the firm and steady perseverance in one great plan, cost the enemy the flower of one of his finest armies without a single general action.

It is not my object to descant with minuteness or military accuracy upon this extraordinary campaign; and I only mention it from its forming so prominent and interesting a feature in the subject before us. The powerful means resorted to by the enemy, his selection of a general supposed to be the favoured child of fortune, his haughty boastings, and rapid strides towards the subjugation of the country, the sad predictions and fears of the people in England, and the invincible firmness with which Lord Wellington (who in opinion almost stood alone,) viewed the gathering storm on the frontier of that country entrusted to his care, are still in the recollection of the public. The rapid and imposing advance of Massina very much alarmed the government and people of Lisbon; and when it was known that his cannon was almost within hearing, terror arrived at its height. The applications for departures and passages to England, America, and almost every part of the globe, became importunate and incessant. The packets, intended to accommodate thirty or forty, were bespoken for from two to three hundred, and confusion and alarm reigned throughout that populous city.

At this time Marshal Beresford was advanced to the Order of the Bath; and, though it may appear singular, the ceremony of his investment and the gaieties attendant upon it actually allayed the storm of anxiety, and appeased the fears of the Portuguese. Lord Wellington gave a grand dinner and ball in the palace of Mafra to the officers and gentry, in honor of the ceremonial of investment. The dinner was of course confined to persons of the highest description, though the invitations to the evening were nearly general. The enemy, amounting to upwards of 80,000 men, was then before us, the out-posts were close, and our allied videttes and his could shake hands. A very small portion of officers only were left in the first line, all the rest being allowed to join in the festivities of the day. Arrangements were however made that every one should return to his post after the ball. The whole of this fearless and judicious measure inspired confidence, and produced a most happy effect. The Portuguese naturally felt, that, if the Commander of the Forces could give a fête to the whole army when a powerful enemy's advanced posts were almost within hearing of his revels, the danger could not be very pressing. It being usual on bespeaking a passage in the packet to pay half down in the event of not going, many of the captains, in consequence of the tranquillity and security diffused through out the city by this well-timed entertainment, acquired considerable property. One of them had absolutely received money from about 250 persons who were flying to England, but who subsequently to this ball altered their resolution; and the captain only carried thirty, the rest forfeiting their deposit rather than adhere to determinations made during the phrenzy of terror and despair.

I having thus given you an hasty sketch of these celebrated lines and of the important purposes they were intended to fulfil, I shall now return to my narrative.

Overhanging Villa Franca (a neat little town near the lines upon the highroad,) stands a mountain which a day's halt gave me an opportunity of ascending, and my pains were well rewarded by the prospect it commanded. A mountainous tract stretching from east to west to an immense extent lay behind me, and the meanderings of the Tagus for many leagues, with a large morass in front, occupied a space farther than the eye could reach; altogether presenting to the view a country which, if properly regulated, would produce a degree of wealth greatly exceeding the present wants of its possessors. The flocks of wild fowl upon the morass, which is partially drained and very thinly peopled, surpass all belief. These parts are also said to be well stocked with game, and I observed numerous birds of prey, such as vultures, a very large species of kite &c. hovering about the cliffs.

A telegraph is erected upon the mountain I have just described, forming an extensive point of communication with Lisbon and other important military stations.

The principal town through which we passed was Santarem, the last stage but one to this place, where we crossed the river by boats. It is a considerable town situated partly upon the summit of an high hill, and partly below it, by the side of the river. From its elevated position, it is considered a very healthy spot, and accordingly is appropriated as a depot for sick and wounded officers, and some large convents are made use of as hospitals in which sixteen hundred men can be accommodated if necessary. From its vicinity to the water also it forms a convenient depot for the business of the commissariat.

I was much pleased with the beauty of a neighbouring view,

which is remarkably woody, and very much resembles the finest views in Surrey. Few of the houses of this town are in a perfect state, but the inhabitants carry on a considerable deal of internal commerce, and most of the necessaries and comforts of life may be purchased among them. The streets are narrow and dirty, but the churches and convents are magnificent. A fine old Moorish castle, still in good repair, overhangs a precipice adjacent to the town, and commands a beautiful and extensive prospect. This fortress possesses a subterraneous passage leading farther than I dared to pursue it, probably originally used as an ambuscade.

I shall abstain from detailing an exact account of every village and town we may have passed through on our march, and shall reserve my remarks for those only which are distinguished by any peculiarity, and refer you more particularly to the map for our route to this place.

Chamusca is a pleasant little town built in a very rich and fertile country, surrounded by hills, covered with the most beautiful heaths flourishing with peculiar luxuriance, which, intermingled with wild lavender, and. other sweet herbs, spread a most agreeable perfume throughout the neighbouring atmosphere.

The Tagus, which winds by the town, affords some small fish, and a species of salmon of a lesser kind than that known in England, altogether indeed of a different species, and in great abundance. Its shape is less round than the English salmon, its colour paler, its flesh softer and more oily, and it contains innumerable small bones. It is however highly prized by the natives, and is not (in the absence of better) refused by us. The river at this place is for the most part shallow, though its depth varies considerably being a few leagues hence totally unnavigable, though very deep within short distances of obstructions.

It is singular that in winter it has less water in it than at other seasons, excepting immediately following the heavy rains. In summer, owing probably to the great increase it receives from the melted snow which descends from the mountains, it is usually fullest.

The inhabitants of this town, as well as those whom we met with on the march, are as hospitable and civil as the nature of their limited means will allow; and they universally appear to be more simple in their manners and inclined to good offices than those in and around the metropolis. A few persons of good property reside in this place and farm their estates, the chief produce of which is wine.

As far as my experience goes beyond the capital, there is more of virtue, cleanliness and industry in the country than in Lisbon and its environs. The manufacture of coarse cloth forms the principal employment of the people during the day, their evenings being spent in mirth and hilarity; while the family, servants, and friends surround the crackling blaze of a cheerful fire-side in the kitchen, the younger persons amusing themselves with dancing to the sound of the guitar, playing at forfeits, or singing.

This fortunate place has not experienced the immediate effects of the enemy's presence; the French army having rested on the opposite banks of the river, making only a few attempts upon their cattle, though never able to gain a footing in the town.

I have now given you a general sketch of this place, and the principal objects on the route. I fancy we are doomed to remain here some time.

Chamusca

Chamusca, March, 1813. During the four or five weeks past the people have been most religiously abstaining from every species of food, which, according to their persuasion, may tend hereafter to shut the door against their entrance into the realms of everlasting happiness; while they have regarded with pity our devouring the lean rations of the commissary as a sensual indulgence too heinous to admit an hope of salvation. I have observed that while my beef-steak was hissing in the frying-pan they thought it no sin to feast their eyes upon it, whatever deadly effect its digestion might have upon their souls; and the eagerness and joy with which they hailed the approaching conclusion of the fast testified the degree of self-denial that this long mortification of their appetites must have cost them. This fast, notwithstanding, is after all less formidable than one might have previously supposed, as the skill shewn in the looking of eggs and fish exemplifies on these occasions. It is indeed proverbial that if you want a good dinner "dine with a priest upon a fast-day."

Processions by torch-light, fire-works, dances, and the more substantial pleasures of the table, awaited the anxious hour of midnight to welcome and usher in the morning of Easter-Sunday, when the fast terminates; at which time the fisher-man lays by his net and the butcher resumes his knife. In the family on which I am billetted a couple of fowls, intended for their supper, performed their evolutions before a blazing fire till the clock had struck the joyful hour, a stewed kid being the first offering that was provided for me on the return of these gratifications; which were hailed with an anticipation of delight scarcely surpassed by Dr. Franklin's friend Keimer, when, after a voluntary abstinence of nearly two years from animal food, he once more found a roasted pig at the free disposal of his knife and fork. The consequences of this long abstinence and sudden repletion, as I have frequently noticed, is, that the people suffer in their health more or less according to the strength of their constitutions. The young and weak are not properly nourished during the fast, and this quick transition few stomachs can bear.

During the interval of spare diet the priests continue to amuse the minds of the people by a variety of ceremonies and processions. Some of these I will relate to you as I literally saw them performed in this place, and which generally indeed prevail throughout the kingdom, in a greater or less degree of splendour, according to the wealth of those who celebrate them. On mid-lent day a long procession sets out from the main church as soon as divine service is finished, with large flags and banners bearing suitable devices; and a figure of Our Saviour larger than life, in the act of carrying the cross, is borne upon the shoulders of the attendants. Priests and assistants in various habits, bearing different insignia and implements, accompanied by musicians, form the procession. Temporary altars are raised in the streets adorned with flowers, and lighted candles (although in broad day-light,) together with all sorts of tawdry tinselled stuff to add to the decoration of the altar. At these places the procession halts, mass is performed, and a pulpit is erected from which a sermon is preached.

I have observed that in most of their discourses they endeavour, by gesticulation and argument, to interest the feelings of the auditors in a manner somewhat resembling that which is pursued by our popular preachers; the whole being very artfully managed, till by gradual steps the priest works himself into a sort of climax almost depriving him of utterance; and the congregation, whether from sympathetic feeling or habit, or in compliment to the priest, seem inspired with an equal degree of enthusiasm, and indeed to a pitch that completely confounded me, and which from its suddenness rendered it absolutely impossible for me to controul an irresistible propensity to indulge my risible faculties. On these occasions, I have seen the preacher unroll a painting during his discourse representing sufferings of Our Saviour, or the death of some martyr, and point to it with feelings that seemed completely to overwhelm him, producing a response of sighs and groans throughout the assembly somewhat resembling the chorus at Smithfield on a market-day. On one of these occasions, while a popular preacher (a monk of the order of Saint Antonio) was addressing a prostrate audience, the figure of an ugly old woman with a silver-leafed tiffany petticoat stretched out on an hoop, and a crescent of tin foil surmounting her head, intended to represent the Virgin Mary, appeared (very apropos) coming round a corner supported upon men's shoulders from a neighbouring church. Instantly the monk in an impassioned strain, and pointing to the figure, made some allusions which at first brought forth repeated and stifled groans from the congregation, succeeded by a loud and sudden yell accompanied with thumping of breasts and smiting of cheeks in a style truly ludicrous. Each party appeared to me to impose equally on the other, and go through the regularly established manoeuvres in a studied and systematic manner; for I could not perceive in this elaborate exhibition, either in the monk (ir his audience, any indication of having in reality suffered from the muteness of their feelings.

Perhaps you may not be aware that sermons are only preached at (Christmas, and upon particular occasions; when the people from all parts of the country flock to the places where these discourses are delivered, dressed in their holiday clothes.

On the night preceding Good-Friday a procession was made by torchlight to all the churches in the town, the object of which appeared to consist in carrying a little figure of Our Saviour, kept in a particular church, to pay its respects to all the other places of worship, in rotation; while at every visit some portion of the service was performed, accompanied by music. At Lisbon I understand this procession is very grand. A silver Jesus is removed from the church of St. Roque to that of the Patriarchs at Bellem, and in former days was attended by the first nobles of the land bare-footed through the streets.

On Good-Friday the procession of the Crucifixion was performed, upon the splendour of which the people greatly prided themselves. Every atom of gold and silver leaf, foil, tinsel, silk, and other finery, with beads, stones, and painted glass, that could be collected, was lent by the inhabitants for the occasion. Children from most families of the place, dressed fantastically with flowers and in the costume of different scriptural characters, assisted at the ceremony. Among these a little urchin with a bundle of sticks at his back represented Isaac, in allusion to his sacrifice. However impossible it may be to suppress a feeling of contempt at such scenes, they must nevertheless produce pity for the gross state of ignorance, and a just sense of indignation for the idolatrous worship which the priesthood inculcates among this superstitious people.

Various other days throughout the year are celebrated in a similar manner, and as the saints are pretty numerous, there is no lack of festivals to keep alive the attention of the people. These saints however (like all public personages) have their existence depending upon popular favour, which, if at all remiss in their duty, is quickly lost. Should any calamity befall a village, the saint whose turn of service it may be for the time being is directly cashiered, and another elected in his room. I was once present at a contested election for the choice of a guardian of this species; the inhabitants of the village being by no means unanimous in their opinion of the merits of the old representative, who was accordingly dismissed, and a new one appointed in his room.

The holidays which succeed a fast have from time immemorial, among other amusements, been celebrated with bull-fights both in Portugal and Spain, and indeed upon the occasion of any public festival. One of these combats I was fortunate enough in having an opportunity of witnessing. The spirit with which they were conducted formerly has fallen off in modern times, and they now afford no specimens of the heroism frequently displayed in ancient days. In Seville and Cadiz I understand they approach nearer to the original mode of managing these entertainments, which are there attended with great risk, and often end fatally. Having heard that a diversion of this species was about to be given by a Portuguese gentleman in the neighbourhood, curiosity prompted me to join the throng, and the result surpassed my expectations. A ring was formed around the gentleman's house by stages, carts &c. the company principally consisting of the numerous peasantry of the neighbourhood. The master of the festival observing several British officers present politely invited us into his house, where an elegant collation was spread, and from the windows we obtained a good view of the combat. The bulls were of a small but strong African breed, and their horns were muffled with short leather caps. Several bulls were provided for the occasion which were brought forward in succession, the same animal in some instances making his appearance more than once upon the stage. This re-entrance usually made the bull more watchful and impatient than others which appeared for the first time before the spectators, though all occasioned excellent sport, considering how much advantage was thrown into the scale of their antagonists. At first I observed that the bull kept the centre of the ring, till repeated provocation induced him to pursue some of his opponents, who were armed with short staves, terminated by a barbed iron point, and capable of entering about one inch into the flesh. Each man carried two of these instruments, and discovered great dexterity in attacking the bull, directing the weapon to the upper and fleshy part of the neck, and returning for the most part unhurt. When the animal is once induced to point his attention to any individual opponent, he is then attacked by the rest; and, when maddened with the quantity of darts by which he is assailed, he is quickly surrounded and forced from the yard into the penn, where the darts are removed and his wounds dressed. Another mode practised in these exhibitions is for the combatants to entice the bull to approach them by a variety of menaces .and gestures, when a cloak is held on one side which the animal eagerly runs at, and disappointed in finding no resistance rolls over upon the ground. A third mode is to meet the bull face to face, and, upon his endeavouring to toss his adversary, the man by a sudden turn and spring seats himself between the two horns, laying hold of each with his hands. A very powerful mulatto was the chief hero of the day and for the sake of the applause bestowed, and occasional present which the spectators threw into the ring, he attempted several dangerous exploits. At one time when he had succeeded in seizing a bull by the horns, it was for a long time doubtful which would prove victorious, as this bull was stronger and more powerful than the rest, and dreadfully enraged at being so handled. The man was repeatedly thrown upon the ground, and again raised from it by the furious animal; till at length the man succeeded in fixing the bull's head (still retaining his hold upon the horns,) so firmly down that he was able to pull the animal completely over, and they both rolled on the ground together without any serious injury to either. Shouts of applause, and showers of vintems and pesetas followed this courageous exertion, and closed the entertainment, which was succeeded by dancing till the weary peasantry dispersed to their homes.

It surprized me to observe among this assemblage of country people, in a nation so much inferior to ours in wealth and knowledge, that the dress and manners of the peasants were infinitely superior, to those of the generality among our peasantry; there being throughout the former a degree of refinement in manners absolutely unknown to the English peasant. Their holiday dress has a gay appearance, consisting usually of a short blue jacket with a quantity of white buttons, breeches of blue, red, or green plush, or cloth, and white cotton stockings, with broad-brimmed, round hats, and a red sash of net-work round the waist. To these they add very large plated buckles to the shoes and knees. Each man usually carries upon all occasions of festivity a long stick in his hand of from seven to eight or nine feet high. With this pole they mount their horses or mules by a spring from the ground. They are extremely expert in the use of it on every occasion, and defy the quickness of a single player. The country people carry this stick as much for defence as for ornament. In the north of Portugal, I am told, they are more expert in the use of these poles than in any other part; where it is also customary to have the lower end of their sticks blackened to the extent of about a foot and an half upwards. The whiteness of their linen and generally cleanly appearance are remarkable, which gives an air of respectability to the crowds assembled upon festive occasions. In their working dress they are less nice, tattered and dirty brown clothes not being despised, nor any contrivance which can be made use of to keep off the effects of inclement weather. Among the latter the most remarkable is a kind of thatched straw great-coat, covering the head and falling over the shoulders and arms, and down below the knees. This is worn by both sexes who are accustomed, in watching the herds, plantations &c. to remain long together in the open air. The first time I saw this I was much astonished and puzzled to understand it. It appeared to me that a little cottage, for I could perceive nothing but this thatch, was moving down the hill; and my horse appeared to be no less surprised, and rather than wait the issue suddenly turned and gallopped back in great terror. The women exhibit grotesque figures from wearing their waists exceedingly long, and their hair piled upon the top of their heads as high as the uncurtailed luxuriance of its growth will admit, sprinkled with flour, and studded with bunches of ribbons; in addition to which they sometimes crown the top with a little black beaver hat. The costume of the higher classes of women approaches nearer to the English taste.

We march to-morrow, and you will hear from me when we take up our next quarters.

Towards Spain

Quadrazais, May, 1813. Soon after I dispatched my last letter we commenced another move inwards headquarters. I am stationed at present in a poor little half-deserted village upon the frontier, within a few miles of Spanish ground. Our march has been long and tedious. During a few days the weather was delightful, but was soon succeeded by almost perpetual hard rains and cold winds, which added to vile roads and billets at miserable habitations, scarcely deserving the name of houses, diminished very greatly the pleasures of our march.

The country throughout this route strongly exhibited the feeble efforts of a people (by nature slothful and prejudiced beyond example,) struggling to recover from the yoke which during many years had oppressed them, and to dissipate the ruin and desolation which the horrors of war have recently scattered over the country, by attending to the arts of husbandry. The soil is naturally prolific and the climate favourable; while the long and uninterrupted sunshine which the country enjoys is relieved by the abundant quantities of water that periodically lull during the rainy seasons, replenishing the numerous springs which perpetually flow from the neighbouring rocks and hills. Here the simplest system of agriculture must flourish, in a land so highly favoured by nature; and were the people industrious, the labour of a few years only would no doubt open a source by which they might ameliorate their condition. But the Portuguese are disinclined to exertion, and suffer the cultivation of vines (of which we reap the advantage,) to occupy the land almost entirely, no great trouble being necessary to their culture. The soil every where also abounds with quantities of stone admirably adapted for the purposes of building, and numerous woods of different species (such as oak, elm, ash, walnut, fir, pines, chestnut, cork &c.) afford timber sufficient in quantity and in quality to supply every purpose for which they can be required. The advantages of pasturage too are very considerable; and the land, generally furnishing admirable feed to the extensive flocks which it is capable of maintaining, with the immense quantities of sweet acorns which every where abound, would, under proper management, sustain innumerable herds of swine &c: good husbandry however must not be looked for in Portugal, till reform has penetrated to the inmost roots of that corruption which undermines the country.

Some few miserable individuals indeed may meritoriously

struggle to obtain a livelihood, or even an independence, but there is generally a want of patriotic spirit and inclination towards improvement throughout the country. The genius of the people appears to be paralysed, and they seem to want energy to take advantage of the relief lately afforded them from French tyranny; and instead of rousing themselves to assert and maintain their natural rights, they still remain a poor, wretched, and oppressed people. How happens it then that this country, possessing such natural advantages and abundant resources in herself, a free trade, a flourishing capital, no enemy threatening its invasion, but on the contrary, a powerful friend in the protection of Great Britain; how happens it that this devoted country still continues so low in its general character and estimation? The answer is obvious—the corrupt government under which they have been so long oppressed has crushed the national pride, and destroyed all emulation among the people to rival other nations, and to adopt and cherish those acquirements, which by enlightening the mind and affording knowledge would naturally augment their power and respectability. But it is not only among the peasantry that the distressed state of the country is observable, but in every other point also.

Literature and general education are not merely at a stand, but actually cannot be said to exist; the fine arts are neglected, and the useful are in practice very far below those of other nations.

Accustomed as we are, and justly, to be proud of eminent advantages which the active and enterprising disposition of the British has insured to the nation, we are rather apt I am afraid to blame, and look down a little too much upon the unfortunate Portuguese. A slight degree of observation and reflection would, I think, convince you that they are rather deserving of pity and commiseration, than of censure and contempt. There does not appear to be any peculiar deficiency of moral principle among the people; and considering the disadvantages under which they labour, their wretched and inefficient government, the haughty and contemptuous conduct of the aristocracy, and the consequent want of all reciprocal feeling between the higher and lower orders, it is matter for astonishment that so many instances of a really virtuous disposition and of native goodness occur, especially in those parts remote from the capital. I think these people in many points of view excel their more proud and arrogant neighbours, who nevertheless affect to despise them. We have seen what the force of British example and discipline, and the appointment of British officers to the Portuguese army have effected. From a nation, heretofore considered as forming the very dregs of Europe, one of the finest, best disciplined and most formidable armies on the Continent has been organised, which I trust will on some future day convince their late Gallic oppressors that they have only "scotched the snake, not killed it." Here then is an instance of what the nation is capable when its power is judiciously directed. May we not, from analogy, fairly suppose an equally beneficial result might attend the cultivation of literature and the arts in general?

From what I have witnessed, I should be led to believe that, were a patriotic monarch placed upon the throne of this country, possessing t lie real interests of his people at heart, much might be effected towards the amelioration of the nation; by cultivating, in the first instance, the friendship of the English, by attending to works of public utility, by stimulating the exertions of the people in the furtherance of arts and sciences, by cherishing literature, and by every possible means holding out for their imitation those pursuits which have led to the greatness of other nations; and, above all, by giving that spring to industry by which these desirable ends can alone be accomplished.

Admitting that the government were thus to interest itself in the welfare of the nation, there can be little doubt, I should conjecture, that the country would ultimately be placed in a situation very opposite to its present degraded state. The disposition of the Portuguese seems submissive and tractable, equally susceptible of a good or a bad direction, according to the nature of the impulse applied.

The great fault, I am afraid, lies in the inherent defects of the government. The character of the present reigning Sovereign is perhaps too well known to call for a detailed description, and the conduct of those acting through his orders partakes of similar deficiencies. Under such circumstances it is natural to suppose that no very great improvement can take place; which indeed has been pretty clearly evinced, by the very slight alteration which the emancipation of the country from French tyranny has occasioned.

It must be granted, that time and considerable attention are required to effect changes in a people placed under their peculiar disadvantages; but, I am convinced that, were a judicious reformation began among those who possess the supreme direction of the nation, the example must of necessity soon be followed throughout every ramification of society. The state of the criminal code is certainly one of the first objects that should be considered, because among all their institutions it is the one most eminently defective; for it is no uncommon event for the innocent and the guilty to suffer alike; nay, the former not unfrequently have been exposed to severe punishment when the latter have wholly escaped.

Their gaols exhibit scenes of wretchedness and filth the most repugnant to every feeling of humanity. No distinction in the degree of crime is observed among the unfortunate prisoners, but all are crowded together in the most loathsome and inhuman manner.

It is a prevailing notion of the uninformed in this country that no faith is to be kept with heretics; an opinion propagated by the ministers of a religion professing to be Christian, while they thus openly violate, by precept and example, the most charitable and essential doctrines of their great master; it is even supposed to be a meritorious act to deprive a Protestant of life, provided it be attended with alledged advantage to their religion.

The use of the stiletto is I believe much less in vogue than in former days, and if a due attention were paid to the internal regulation of the country, no doubt it would soon altogether cease.

With the exception of one or two large towns, all the places that we have passed through are in a state of excessive poverty and desolation; and the few miserable inhabitants that remain, appear to continue their residence more from inability to change than from any advantage attached to their homes. No persons of consequence live among them, in whose service they can advance themselves; and, thus shut out from every stimulus to exertion, they mostly gain a precarious livelihood from the occasional wants of travellers or soldiers accidentally passing.

The French army in its passage through this country has probably fully satiated its predominant propensity to rob, plunder, and commit every sort of atrocity which unrestrained military power is but too prone to license. The history of these atrocities is almost unparalleled, and shocks every feeling of humanity. During their retreat they set on fire cities, towns, and villages, and the allied armies in the course of their pursuit entered not only the beautiful city of Leireira in flames, but almost every town and village in the line of march; while peasants hanging upon trees, priests and whole families murdered in their houses, and others lying dead by the road side, exhibited dreadful witnesses of the savage conduct of their relentless invaders. The Portuguese on their parts however have occasionally not been backward in retaliation, when opportunities occurred of revenging their wrongs; for revenge is a feeling innately connected with the Portuguese character, which their state of society is ill calculated to abate. Upon the breaking up of the French army from before Lisbon, when it was closely pressed upon by the allies, the first care of those who were unable to keep up with the retreating columns was to endeavour to fall into the hands of the British, whose name they justly held in estimation for generosity and forbearance to their enemies; while they well knew what they had to expect, and indeed richly deserved, from submitting themselves to the power of the Portuguese. The Portuguese peasantry were every where lying in wait for those unfortunate stragglers, many of whom fell into their hands, and deaths of the most cruel kind were on such occasions the inevitable result. Two out of the numerous instances that occurred I will relate to you. During the retreat through the province of Beira some Frenchmen, unable to keep up, were attacked by the infuriated peasantry armed with long sticks, fire-arms &c. who overpowered and captured them; the mercy of instant death was denied, and so good an opportunity of satiating their revenge was not overlooked by the Portuguese. The prisoners were bound and conducted to the summit of the great Estrella, where they were tortured in various ways, and ultimately stoned to death. On another occasion, whilst the enemy was before our position in front of Lisbon, a French escort consisting of three dragoons with a female in company, and all mounted, was passing through the village of Faya; the armed peasants surrounded them in the market place and captured them. The unfortunate party supplicated for mercy on their knees, giving up their money, clothes and provisions to save their lives. Their relentless enemies kept them for a while alive, deriding their miseries, sporting with the horrors of their situation, and perpetually promising their lives as each boon was surrendered; till at length, stript naked and lying prostrate before them, they actually beat out all their brains, reserving the woman as the last sufferer. This revengeful feeling was not unfrequently gratified in Spain, but throughout Portugal it was universal, and though to be regretted certainly helped to further the great cause. The inveteracy of the peasantry proved an excellent ally to the British general; for the French by their cruelties unquestionably worked against themselves; and according to the established rules of retributive justice, the inhumanities of which they were guilty were thus ultimately visited upon their own heads. Dreadfully however as the Portuguese suffered under the tyranny of their late oppressors, it would have been better for them to have remained in this lamentable situation than have continued under the imbecile and wretched despotism of their old government, not improved or ameliorated by experience of the late striking events.

In my professional capacity it has fallen to my lot to visit the poorest and most distressed classes; and miserable as the state of this order of society appears to be upon a casual view of it, it is yet nothing when compared with that which is furnished by a more intimate acquaintance with its evils. Often destitute of hospitals, and without the aid of medical men, the unfortunate victims linger in the most loathsome and deplorable state which poverty and disease can indict, and are consequently doomed to drag out their miserable existence a burthen to their families and to themselves. I found the little assistance I was enabled to afford them was eagerly sought and very gratefully accepted, and as the intelligence of the opportunity of relief spread abroad, the numbers of the afflicted, and the excess to which their various diseases had reached by neglect, astonished me. Whenever I met with medical men 1 uniformly found their science limited to a degree which almost exceeds belief. Their study is chiefly confined to the perusal of a few old authors, whose practice among us has become obsolete; and they have consequently few conceptions beyond the dogmas of the latter. The surprise they evinced at the surgical apparatus of an English medical officer, and at the commonest operations, proved the lamentable state of the whole profession in Portugal. The people in general, as well as the medical practitioners, are in perpetual terror of infection, for they are wholly ignorant of its nature and the most common ways of preventing it. Even to this day the Portuguese cherish an invincible prejudice against the use of mercury, in cases where we know of no other remedy to check the progress of disease. Their prejudice against vaccination was equally strong, but by the interference of the legislature it has been introduced; and the arrival of vaccine matter from England is occasionally announced in the Gazette, and inoculation performed gratuitously.

From what I have mentioned, you have probably by this time a pretty just idea of the extreme deficiency of this nation, in every essential which can tend to place it on a level with the more civilized states of modern Europe.

On the March

Quadrazais, May, 1813. The picture which I have given in my last letter of the Portuguese is probably extremely different from the one which you have naturally imbibed in England, but it is nevertheless a true one. Let us however leave so disagreeable a subject, and proceeding to the more favourable side of the picture, turn to the numerous beauties every where to be met with in journeying through this delightful country. Nature has been lavish in the distribution of her bounties over the face of the land, which every where presents objects grateful to the senses. The eye is pleased with an infinite variety of verdure and foliage, and the wild and irregular forms which she has bestowed upon the earth, present romantic as well as picturesque scenery in every direction. It would be well worth a botanist's while to make a tour through Portugal in the early spring. Many of the finest plants, preserved in our gardens with the nicest care, are here considered of no account, and constantly liable to be trodden under foot as matters deserving no attention. When the flowers are in blossom the air is perfumed with a variety of aromatic plants, among which the heaths are most conspicuous, and grow for the most part with peculiar strength and luxuriance. The geranium, and some few others are met with only in detached spots, but the arbutus, the gum-cystus &c. are almost every where to be found in great profusion. In the country about Niza (which place I shall have occasion to mention to you as lying in our late route,) the hills and plains are covered with the latter plant, growing very luxuriantly and to a great height. The almond and wild peach-trees afford the strongest and sweetest scents and the most beautiful blossoms, far surpassing those of any other description of plants, perfuming the air to a great extent. The orange, lemon and lime-trees produce also blossoms of the most beautiful description. In addition to the common acid lemon another sort is generally to be met with of a sweet but rather vapid flavour. The oranges in like manner differ very materially in their qualities, but every sort is more pleasant and wholesome when eaten off the tree, than when kept in store for a long time. With this exception, and perhaps some few others, I think the generality of our fruits are more palatable, especially the grape, arising probably from the greater degree of attention which is paid to its cultivation among us.

There is very little corn grown in Portugal, and the bread is generally very bad. Indian corn is the most abundant, from its answering so great a variety of purposes. It is made into meal for bread and cakes, and in other respects forms a considerable article of diet. The horses and mules are also fed upon it, while the stalks and leaves maintain the oxen. Mats, beds &c. are likewise made with the straw.—Very little grass is grown in Portugal, the herds living chiefly upon the scanty pasturage of the mountains. Olive-groves and vineyards are almost every where common, oil and wine being the principal articles of consumption and exportation.

In our passage up the country we met with several objects worthy of notice. Occasional vestiges of the Moors, and sometimes of the Romans, frequently arrested our attention. Towers of the former construction are to be easily distinguished from those of the latter by their square form, the others generally partaking of the circular figure. Near the village of Arripiado, three leagues from Chamusca, situated in the middle of the Tagus, I observed a very ancient specimen of the former description. A few leagues from this place on the opposite side of the river stands the town of Thomar, celebrated for the beauty and richness of the country around it, being in itself a small and neat place.

On the second day of our march we reached Abrantes, a large, populous, and in its general appearance an handsome town, built on the summit of a very lofty hill over the Tagus, and commanding fine and extensive views. The road to it winds through an interesting and romantic country. The river is broad and deep at this place, and a bridge of boats is thrown over it, which communicates with the town and its extensive suburbs on either side. It is by nature strong, and art has not been spared to improve its position. The best part of the town consists in an irregular open space where the market is held, but the streets are all narrow, dirty, and confined, and the houses generally bad. It forms a great depot for the army, which gives it an appearance of liveliness and bustle otherwise not natural to it.

The next considerable town in our route is Niza, situated in a fine elevated plain, and formerly surrounded by a strong Roman fortification. It is now in bad repair and thinly peopled. The tower and parts of the chambers, and the wall of an ancient Roman castle are still left, and the remains of a strong wall nearly surround the town. It is a confined and dirty place, and contains only a few tolerable houses.

About this neighbourhood we found less cultivation than in those districts through which we had recently passed, and for a time we took our leave of olives, grapes, oranges, and almost every other production of the soil. The wine here is in consequence very bad and dear, being much adulterated with water and a strong ardent spirit, called *agua ardiente*, made from the grape after it has been pressed for the manufacture of wine, and constituting the brandy of the Portuguese. This, combined with the pitchy flavor the wines often acquire from the pig-skins, creates a mixture which the stomach even of a British soldier cannot bear.

During our march between this place and a little wretched deserted village called Sarnadas, we crossed the Tagus at the celebrated pass of Villa Velha, so called from a very neat little town of that name in the neighbourhood. Our road lay over a barren and craggy range of rocks, forming a constant succession of hill and dale, till we arrived at the edge of the precipices, beneath which the Tagus winds its serpentine course; the country on the opposite side appearing verdant, woody and cultivated. The river has here evidently forced its way between a sierra, as the former connection between the two sides may be traced with the greatest ease, and many similar instances occur in Portugal. The descent of the above pass is by a very narrow and circuitous path. The river is broad and deep about this place, and a temporary bridge of boats has been formed for the passage of troops. The boats with which the bridge was made were brought from Abrantes, over a country apparently impassible to any sort of carriage; yet the quickness with which they were transported reflects the highest credit upon those employed in the undertaking, and forms one among many instances of the energy which characterized every thing emanating from the distinguished chief in command. On the opposite side of the pass we arrived at an elevation of about equal height with that which we had already descended, commanding a fine and extensive prospect from its summit. The appearance of this scenery strongly reminded me of the Severn and St. Vincent's rocks in the neighbourhood of Bristol. Eagles, vultures, storks, and abundance of game are seen in the neighbourhood of Villa Velha, which is beautifully diversified with sloping hills covered with wood and verdure, and backed by a lofty sierra of rocky mountains. Numerous neatly white-washed houses interspersed among the hills, and surrounded by groves, imparted a more cheering prospect than usually attends the great route by which the armies pass.

A few leagues from Villa Velha the populous and thriving town of Castel Branco, occupying a strong position, stands upon an eminence surrounded by extensive suburbs, and commanding a variegated and almost endless prospect. The roads entering the town are impassable in a carriage of any kind, except a bullock-car. The streets are mostly very narrow and dirty, but it possesses a fine open market-place, and the houses are above the ordinary size. The castle (which deserves any thing but its present appellation,) is situated above the town, surrounded by a strong wall and moat. It is I believe from its appearance of Saracenic origin, but no accurate account can be obtained upon such subjects as these from the natives, as they are generally too ignorant to afford any information upon matters more remote than those immediately relating to their own times. Several churches of Gothic architecture are still to be seen in this town, the chief of which is very spacious and handsome, and adorned with some fine paintings. A very elegant palace of red brick with large gardens forms the residence of the bishop. Unfortunately this fine place became during the early periods of the war the seat of plunder and desolation, many traces of which are still visible, and among others a very valuable library, in common with the palace itself, suffered materially.

The fortifications surround the greater part of the town, and are furnished with draw-bridges &c. though not in the best repair. The country about this neighbourhood is better cultivated than that which we recently quitted on the other side of the Tagus; and a large quantity of wine is made in the vicinity, notwithstanding the country becomes more mountainous, particularly approaching Sabugal; which town about two years ago was the scene of a severe contest and much bloodshed. It stands (like most of the towns of Portugal) upon an eminence, in the midst of an open and hilly country, still retaining vestiges of ancient fortifications, an old ruined castle, surrounded by a very deep fosse and a strong wall. The condition of the town occasioned me great disappointment. Before you enter the place it wears the appearance of prosperity and comfort; but on a nearer approach it is found to be a perfect ruin, nearly desolate, poor beyond description, and almost entirely incapable of affording accommodation in a sufficient state of repair to prevent the rain (which when I was there was intense,) from pouring on one's bed through the roof.

I have now brought you nearly to the frontiers, and shall in my succeeding letter commence my remarks upon Spain; for were I to enter more at large upon a description of Portugal and its inhabitants, it would only prove a recapitulation of the disgusting, and unsatisfactory account which I have already given you of desolated and ruined houses, and an impoverished and miserable people, with the means of happiness in their possession, though with a total incapacity to make use of the blessings and natural advantages they possess. In the sketch I have taken you will perhaps think me too laconic; but to describe a country like this, under its present circumstances, must require a longer residence than I have had among the people, to enable me to enter more fully upon the subject.

Salamanca

Salamanca, May, 1813. I write to you from this celebrated, beautiful, and formerly flourishing city, where we have been a few days, and of which, when I have taken a little more time to examine it, I shall be able to give you a more perfect account. In the meanwhile let me lead you back to the frontiers, which I have so recently quitted, and over which I sincerely hope never to be obliged to retrace my steps.

It is an observation which I have very generally heard mentioned, by every one entering Spain directly from Portugal, that the difference between the general aspect of the two countries, and the manners and appearance of the natives, even close to their respective borders, is much more striking than it is possible to imagine; when it is considered that, the exact limits are so far from being defined as to be quite imaginary. The roads, the houses, and the general features of the country, all differ materially in their appearance with a very manifest advantage in favour or Spain. The inhabitants of the latter are much cleaner, better dressed, and altogether neater and more industrious, and exhibit greater tokens of civilization in their domestic concerns.

One of the chief objects worthy of notice, on entering the first village across the frontier, consists in the difference between the Spanish and Portuguese bread; the latter being execrable, and the former very fine. Nature has evidently done much for the Spaniards, and they certainly make a better use of her gifts than the Portuguese.

The lower orders live in small, comfortable, white-washed cottages, and instead of decayed and dirty old boarded floors, stone or brick ones are substituted, tending to keep their houses cool, and free from vermin, which swarm in those of the Portuguese.

On all sides indications of industry are to be met with. Small gardens are attached to every house which can admit of such a convenience, and pains are taken in their cultivation, as well as in the care of poultry and flocks. It is nevertheless true that the country people are not very prosperous; on the contrary, much poverty reigns among them; but they have energy "to force the trade of life" to a degree very much above their neighbours, and are not sunk in despair like the miserable peasantry of the Portuguese.

In giving this decided preference to the Spaniards, I must be understood to embrace objects merely relating to civilization and the comforts of life. The regard which the Portuguese entertain for the English is far from being equally felt by the Spaniards; for in this point of view the Portuguese greatly excel their neighbours; and were they to live only a little more like civilized beings I should prefer their character to that of the Spaniards.

The roads through which we have marched are all excellent, and are capable of being passed in carriages, with the exception of some bye-roads, which are very similar to the stony lanes to be met with in some parts of England. The royal roads leading to this town and thence to Madrid, Burgos &c. are wide, smooth, and handsome, and scarcely excelled by any in our own country; all their roads are flanked, to a considerable distance round the town, with rows of fine trees, which form a great shelter from the intense heat to which this open part of the country is commonly exposed.

I have enjoyed this last march very much, the weather having been uninterruptedly clear, rendering bivouacking in the woods delightful, and the surrounding country much more pleasing to my eye than that to which it had recently been accustomed.

The snow-topped mountains, rocks, ravines, and cataracts have gradually disappeared from our view as we advanced into Spain, and are succeeded by abundance of wood, rich pasturage and fertile cornfields, with no greater elevation of land than occasionally a gentle slope.

A very elegant species of dwarf-oak, with a frosted silvery appearance, is much cultivated, and forms by far the greatest portion of the wood about these parts. The acorn they produce is very delicate in flavor, and is much used in deserts, and forms a principal article of food among the poorer classes, being finer than the common species of sweet acorn. The pigs which feed upon them are greatly prized for the delicacy of their flesh. Firs, pines, poplars, beech, walnut-trees &c. are also very common.

The first Spanish town of note which we passed was the celebrated Ciudad Rodrigo. It is a very handsome, neat little city, built upon a slight eminence. The streets for the most part are small and narrow, but very clean, and the houses in general are good. It has all the appearance internally of a thriving place, but its walls without still retain many vestiges of the dreadful convulsions in which it had been recently engaged.

The churches, and other public buildings, are very elegantly constructed; and the former being ornamented with carving about their porticos, and surmounted with domes and turrets, give an imposing and pleasing appearance to the town; while its position, and its strong fortifications, must ever render it an important station between contending armies, under the circumstances attendant upon those recently engaged in the Peninsula.

The suburbs of Ciudad Rodrigo are very extensive, and probably exceed the town itself in magnitude; which added very much to the comforts of our armies lying before the town during the sieges.

Lord Wellington honored this city with a visit on re-entering Spain, and was received with every demonstration of exultation and respect. He gave a grand ball and supper to the inhabitants, and amused them with the ceremony of investing General Cole with the Order of the Bath.

On the day previous to our entering Salamanca, three thousand of the enemy were surprised by our advanced posts, who charged them over the bridge, and drove them through the streets out of the town; and, following them over the downs on their way to Burgos, took three hundred prisoners, and killed between fifty and sixty men, principally by means of the artillery.

The French General commanding (Villette,) was leisurely walking through the streets with his mistress, when the alarm was given of the approach of the British. He made his escape with difficulty, but the lady and the carriage fell into our hands.

Curiosity induced me to follow the tracks by which the enemy retired, and while thus employed I met with many of the bodies of the killed lying in different directions, mangled most dreadfully by cannon-shot. Many had been buried by the inhabitants of a neighbouring village, and those which remained had become victims to wolves and birds of prey.

On my return I was much surprised by encountering a numerous flock of vultures, of a very large size. They appeared to have been disturbed by my approach, and had in consequence rendezvoused in a retired and sheltered position under a piece of rising ground, till my departure afforded them an opportunity of again regaling at their ease upon their horrible repast. My coming so suddenly upon them completely deceived me as to their nature, for, till they arose into the air (literally darkening it by their numbers,) I supposed them to be an herd of goats. Some Spaniards informed me that similar bands of these depredators occasionally prove formidable to a solitary passenger, for that when they are pressed by hunger they are sometimes known to attack him, and without ceremony devour him. I leave you to judge of the truth of this, although I do not conceive it to be altogether impossible.

Lord Wellington attended by his staff and several British and Spanish generals, with Castanos, (the Generalissimo of the Spanish army,) remained in Salamanca a short time; during which dinners, balls, and suppers were given, and the whole party appeared one evening at the theatre.

The morning after the French had been driven away a grand *Te Deum* was performed at the cathedral—which was attended by Lord Wellington, the generals &c. and produced a very interesting effect. This cathedral is usually considered as one of the first in Spain. It is built of a kind of white freestone, surmounted with elegant turrets, bastions, arches, and a large dome, and adorned with a profusion of carving and varieties of fancy-work, scriptural histories &c. in a most rich and elaborate style. It is a very lofty and spacious edifice, standing in an open square, surrounded by railing. Its external beauties exceed those of its interior, though the latter is very superior when compared with most others. The grand altar is very magnificent, opposite to which stands the chancel, greatly resembling those in our cathedrals. These are surrounded by a screen of stone-work exquisitely carved. The edifice contains two organs in the gallery, one of which is remarkable for its size and superior tone. The church also, from its munificent endowments, is able to maintain a very superior band of singers from Italy. This venerable building was lately threatened with destruction by their late barbarous invaders. Some of the usually levied contributions could not (from a total deficiency of means) be discharged, and the French general in consequence threatened by way of intimidation to destroy the cathedral, unless his unreasonable demands were complied with. The reply returned was—that, as it was public property, it did not effect the personal interests of individuals like their other exorbitant levies, and that therefore no one would interfere; the arrival however of the English prevented the accomplishment of this tyrannical threat of the French general, if indeed it were ever seriously intended to be put into execution.

The situation of Salamanca for so large and populous a city commands many advantages, and in whatever point of view it is taken, it wears the appearance of an handsome and flourishing town. The Tormes, which is a clear and wide river, but in many places very shallow, winds round two-thirds of the town, while the elevation of western part of the city from its banks renders it an airy and very healthy place. An excellent light red wine called Vino de Tormes is made on the banks of this river. Vines are not cultivated in the immediate vicinity of Salamanca, the land being chiefly dedicated in these parts to corn. The natural position of Salamanca is strong, and some pains have been taken to secure it by a substantial wall built around it, which in its most exposed situation is flanked by a strong bastion. The streets for the most part are narrow, but the houses are very lofty and generally pretty good. Some of the former are well paved, and kept tolerably clean. From the abundance of shops of all descriptions a great retail trade is apparently carrying on. The city contains also a very well supplied market, which is held in an open space where the municipal house is erected. The principal square forms one of the handsomest I have seen in Spain, the houses being constructed of white stone, built very high, with great regularity, and supplied with balconies and large green virandas to the windows, which add much to the liveliness of their appearance. Piazzas are erected over the broad pavement round the square, forming the great resort of fashionable society, when the weather will not permit promenading round the '*Prado del Toro*,' situated without the eastern walls of the town. Varieties of shops, excellent coffee-houses, billiard-rooms &c. are to be met with under these piazzas, which may be considered as forming the Bond-street of Salamanca. The general appearance of the city, and the number of large and handsome houses which are seen in different parts, might lead to the supposition of its being very rich and peopled. But this is far from being the case, for on a closer inspection it is found to be extremely deficient, and indeed scarcely amounts to a third of its former wealth and population. The inhabitants have become greatly impoverished, and the owners of the principal residences have either absolutely left the country altogether, and followed the fortunes of Joseph Buonaparte, or have removed to other towns of greater safety, such as Valladolid &c. so that few people of the higher ranks of society are now resident in the place.

The towns-people are in general hospitable and communicative. They have their *tertulias*, or evening assemblies, when they converse, play cards, dance or sing; and they also pretty constantly frequent the theatre, which is a light and elegant building and fitted up somewhat in the style of the Opera-house in London, though very inferior with respect to size, while the actors and performances are below mediocrity. The present appearance of the town excites many melancholy reflections, when contrasted with the accounts which we have been accustomed to receive of its former magnificence, and high reputation as a seat of learning. Neither Oxford, nor Cambridge, I am convinced, from the appearance of the colleges (the walls of which are still standing,) equal in any point of view what this once flourishing town exhibited in better days. Perhaps you will not think me guilty of exaggeration, when I tell you that there are still the remains of nineteen splendid colleges, built of an handsome white stone, most elaborately and classically ornamented, forming once one of the chief repositories of ancient literature, which subsequently enlightened modern Europe. Several of these colleges were dedicated entirely to Irish students, numbers of whom are to be met with in the church, the army, and various other departments of the state, who have now become naturalized, and constitute perhaps the best informed part of the community.

The chief aim of the French, during their residence in this country, appears to have been the annihilation of the government of Spain, (of which they hoped, to have obtained the entire control), by introducing an alteration in the manners and customs of the people more congenial with their own views; pursuing, in this respect, a very opposite policy from that which they practised in Portugal; that, being a country over which they could scarcely ever hope to reign with unlimited sway, was treated more in the light of a conquered kingdom, and rapine and devastation were committed wherever they went. Thus, in the former instance, every old establishment was destroyed; and, while they secured the King and frightened the government into obedience, they annihilated the influence of the priests, and abolished all religious and learned institutions with remorseless rigour. Those walls which, during the prosperous days of Spain, contained all that is estimable in science and literature, are now converted into receptacles for the passing armies, alternately preying upon the vitals of the country.

What a lesson has Spain been taught; what a check given to the pride of a people, once the first in the world, and now sunk into poverty and meanness! And yet, how has this lesson been thrown away! For, to hear a Spaniard talk, and to read the manifestos which are from time to time published, it would appear that Spain is now in the very zenith of its glory, and that the chivalrous high former days still existed with undiminished lustre. But, it is lamentable to remark, that pride, selfishness, and what may be called the vices only of those illustrious times, are all that remain to the once lofty and dignified character of the Spanish nation. Conscious of what they have been, the Spaniards are content to live upon their former reputation, retaining all their ancient pride without an atom of their former merit.

In addition to the ruined colleges, the town contains several convents and monasteries equally spacious and magnificent, one or two of which are still in a sufficiently good repair to afford an asylum to a few religious and decayed orders.

Awaiting Orders

Salamanca, May, 1813. We have been in daily expectation of an order to march, having understood that there is no probability of our halting before the army reaches Burgos, where it is generally supposed the chief struggle will take place. The experience of the last year at this position has probably given the enemy more confident hopes and expectations than appear likely to be realized.

So far as I can judge, from the very slender military knowledge which my limited means of observation afford, no army ever set out in finer condition than ours on this occasion. It is exceedingly healthy, and has had time to refresh itself; while the unfortunate check it met with last year seems to have redoubled its ardor and confidence, instead of producing an opposite effect.

The infantry are well provided with tents in the present campaign; which so greatly adds to the health and comfort of the soldier, that it must necessarily prove a powerful assistance in preserving the strength of every regiment that, in former campaigns, was so greatly reduced by sickness, fatigue, and extreme exposure to the weather. In addition to this may be added the sense that government now entertains of the necessity of considerably reinforcing this army; and that the Spaniards seem at last to be alive to the policy of adequately meeting the present emergency; though, I must say, with regard to the latter acquisition, it is generally considered as a consoling reflection, that, "in case of accidents, we can do without their assistance".

With the Portuguese army every one appears highly satisfied; but the general appearance of the Spanish forces is by no means prepossessing. Falstaff's troops which he was ashamed to conduct through Coventry form a tolerably fair picture of most of their corps.

I had the curiosity to mingle with the admiring crowd yesterday assembled without the walls, to witness a Spanish review by Castanos. The Generalissimo, gorgeously arrayed, was mounted upon a black Andalusian horse in a full suite of white laced regimentals, surrounded by his staff in blue uniforms, and escorted by a troop of Royal Lancers clothed in yellow. There were from five to six thousand men upon the ground. An inspection of necessaries formed one part of the ceremony, of which, from motives of curiosity alone, I wished to be a spectator. Had the men all been marched through Monmouth-street, in order that every one might suit himself according to his taste, it is hardly possible to suppose a selection more ridiculously happy, than the assemblage I then witnessed, as to shape, colour, and quality.

I remember once hearing a story of the commandant of an Irish corps of volunteers, who, after appointing a parade for inspecting the clothing of his regiment, ordered that those who possessed shirts and breeches should form the front rank, those with breeches and no shirts the centre, and those without either the rear; but I believe it would have puzzled the Irish colonel to muster any other rank, throughout the whole of this very picturesque review, than the last mentioned.

Notwithstanding the great deficiency of appointment and discipline, in this army, the men are naturally fine looking fellows, and if well organized, clothed, and officered, would no doubt prove a formidable force.

The officers in general are wretched and miserable in their appearance, their dress is not often better than that of the men, and equally irregular and unmilitary. I have often seen them eating and drinking, and conversing familiarly with the privates; and it is not unusual to meet an officer riding, in good fellowship, with one of them upon the same mule, the animal bearing the personal baggage of his two riders, rarely equalling the scanty allowance even of the Honorable Mr. Dowlas in the 'Heir at Law.'

Our stay at this place has given me time to wander about its vicinities, and I was much interested the other day on being shewn, by an officer who was present in the battle, the different positions of the two armies engaged last year upon these memorable plains. The view of the engagement from the heights near the town must have been very grand and striking, as it comprehended, from the great expanse of country, the whole extent of the positions of the contending armies. The field of battle retains no apparent vestiges of this great engagement, as it is now entirely covered with corn, in which the whole country abounds. This, among numerous other instances, shows the great fertility of the soil; for no pains were spared by the enemy to prevent the re-growth of the corn. The wheat grown here is remarkable for its height, and is generally of a very fine quality, far exceeding what I have ever seen before. The bread made from it is peculiar, somewhat in substance between biscuit and cake, eats very short, and is close in its texture. It is sold in great abundance in the market-places, in all kinds of shapes, and keeps good a much longer time than any other bread I have ever tasted. In corn provinces it is exceedingly cheap, though, very dear in those part's where corn does not form the stable commodity. You may not perhaps be aware that in Portugal and Spain they do not use barm in making their bread, but leven, which, while it binds the bread to a close texture, by no means creates heaviness. Rye is mixed occasionally in a greater or less degree with the wheat, and forms an inferior kind of bread, liable quickly to become assescent and unwholesome.

The Fording of the Douro

Palencia, June, 1813. An order suddenly arriving for the brigade to move on obliged me to finish my last letter abruptly. Our course has been along the road to Burgos, which being a '*camino real*,' or royal road, was, as usual, in very excellent order.

We marched into this town about two o'clock to-day; and the confusion, occasioned by the whole army concentrating at this place, has hurried my ideas to a degree from which they are scarcely yet recovered; but, as we expect to move on tomorrow, I am desirous to finish this letter before I retire to rest. A large force of the enemy recently occupied the town, where their head-quarters were established, and which were removed by the flight only of King Joseph, so late as yesterday evening at five o'clock, and some of their cavalry even did not get clear of the town till twelve o'clock this morning. The people appear to be unfeignedly rejoiced at our arrival, as the enemy, during their stay, kept them in great awe and fear; and they have in this short interval been much busied in opening their shops and stores, where wines &c. were concealed, for the accommodation of our troops; a precaution very necessary, for had the French soldiers discovered those hordes, they would inevitably have seized them by force, and applied them to their own purposes, without troubling themselves to remunerate the unfortunate owners.

As it was expected that the enemy would make a stand at this place, the three great divisions of the army concentrated around the town, part of the cavalry and the staff being quartered within its walls, and the rest encamped on the plains around.

The day was very fine, which, together with the extent and openness of the country, presented a very grand and pleasing prospect, rendered more interesting from the liveliness occasioned by the arrival of the combined armies. The concourse of mules, carrying the baggage of the army, and the various camp followers, occupied more than treble the space of the army itself, and presented a moving scene so far as the eye could reach on all sides. The town is large, but it has a shabby look and an air of poverty, though when viewed from a distance it assumes a fine appearance.

It has a large cathedral church, which, though plain in its external appearance, is nevertheless very handsomely and elaborately ornamented on the inside; the city contains also several convents, which have escaped injury, inhabited by nuns; these buildings are spacious, but their establishments are very poor.

Near the skirts of the town, and occupying a space little less than that of the town itself, stand the remains of the once magnificent and wealthy convent of Saint Francisco; which, about six years ago, attracted the jealousy and cupidity of Buonaparte, who was unwilling to suffer an order so rich and powerful to exist; and accordingly, not content with ruining the splendid establishment, caused eighteen unfortunate friars to be surrounded, and put to death in the cloisters. A lay-brother, a venerable old man, who was under-librarian to the house, and who still remains in charge of the little property left by the plunderers, related to me, with tears in his eyes, and a just expression of indignation, the account of this cruel murder, of which he himself was a melancholy witness.

If a monastic life can possess any charm they certainly must be found in such a convent as the one I am now describing. Whatever may have been the self-denial of its occupiers at particular times and occasions, the leading system bears no traces of abstinence and mortification, but rather resembles that of the palace of Epicurus himself.

A large proportion of the convent still remains, in spite of the devastation it has sustained. Remnants of costly furniture, and beds, somewhat less hard than those I remember to have seen in a convent in Dorsetshire, which was inhabited by monks of the order of Le Trappe, are still in existence, remaining in every quarter of the building. The establishment appears formerly to have included an extensive library, most of the books belonging to which have been recently carried away, the remainder lying about the rooms without order and in confused heaps. The offices are spacious and convenient, and the halls, refectory, and chapel bespeak the former splendor of the institution. I have uniformly found, on our advance from Salamanca, that the population of the country increases. The district about Palencia is extensive and well peopled, villages are seen in all directions, and they are for the most part very thickly inhabited; which is far from being the case nearer the Portuguese frontiers. The country we are now in is open, very much exposed, and furnished with little wood, though abounding with corn of every description. A small quantity of wine is also made in the neighourhood. I was informed by the inhabitants that the French officers went off in full confidence of a speedy return; that they said we should remain there a short time, and drink the favourite English beverage rum, and then very shortly take our departure to the rear again. I think, however, that they are mistaken, for the probability is that they are not likely to see this place again; unless as prisoners. I am afraid you will think, while I am dwelling upon this town, that I am perhaps forgetting those which we must necessarily have passed through upon our route from Salamanca; after quitting which, we occasionally halted among fine woods and small villages. The most interesting military movement which occurred upon our march was the fording of the river Douro, under the walls of Toro. The city of Toro is to all appearance by nature impregnably fortified on the western side, and certainly not deficient in defence on every other, the whole being surrounded by an exceedingly strong and high wall.

The enemy a few days since destroyed the bridge, which, as they supposed, must secure them from our pursuit; and their astonishment could have been scarcely greater than our own, upon finding the many advantages which the city possessed no barrier to the progress of the allied forces; these formidable means of opposition proving a very slight obstacle only to the advancing army; for the enemy's right and left being quickly turned in succession, they were compelled instantly to retire before the overwhelming force of the combined army. The river at this place is very deep, and flows with a rapid stream, the force of which is increased by a circuitous course. A little below the bridge is a fordable passage for cavalry, the immense body of which passing at one time assisted greatly to stem the torrent, though it forced them to pursue a diagonal rather than a direct course. A small proportion only of the horses could keep their legs, the rest being obliged absolutely to swim through the torrent. Other portions of the army crossed the Ezla; and these fordings proved fatal to many, though not perhaps to the degree which might reasonably have been expected, from the difficulties attending this passage. The city of Toro is small, but neat, handsome, and compact, and its appearance when viewed from a distance is very imposing. For the spot on which the bridge lately stood, and which is again erecting, a wide and excellently gravelled road runs in a serpentine course to the summit of a very lofty precipice, on the scite of which the city stands; from which all in front is a flat, verdant and quite level country, abounding in villages; while on the opposite side the view is beyond conception fine and extensive, owing to its being a very open and champagne country In the course of our progress we were quartered in the ruins of the convent of Saint Espinos. This building, though in a ruined state, still bears many marks of ancient magnificence. The neighbouring lands which formerly belonged to it are very beautiful, rich, and extensive.

It certainly appears, upon a cursory view, very lamentable to see so many fine establishments become a prey to the existing state of rapine and disorder; though I am inclined to believe that the benefit arising to Spain, from its present disastrous situation, may hereafter prove of essential service to the country.

Towards Vitoria

Salvatierra, June, 1813. Our advance has been so rapid, that little time has been allowed for observation; though, since I wrote to you from Palencia, a detail of the leading features of our progress may not be uninteresting,

With the events that have recently occurred, you will probably have been made acquainted before the receipt of this letter, which I am sure must occasion you the most joyful sensations.

On the 21st of May the army had not advanced beyond the frontier, the enemy occupying all the strong holds of the country. On the 21st of the following month the enemy was beaten and routed, almost as it should seem by magic, and driven to the Pyrenees.

Perhaps in no period of history have so many important, and unlooked-for events been crowded into so short a space of time.

My hopes of seeing Burgos have been frustrated, as the news of the French exploding the city and retiring, arriving while we were approaching to the place, caused our course to be turned more directly northward, through a country unknown hitherto to British troops.

Every step we have advanced has brought daily into view a more mountainous country; the roads however for the most part are very good, and the country generally fertile, while the innumerable villages scattered throughout the provinces, manifest a larger proportion of population, than could have been expected (in the present distracted state of the country) to exist.

Cultivation appears to be carried to a considerable height, though it falls very short of that practised in England.

The inhabitants of those places through which we have passed, regarded our approach with a greater degree of enthusiasm and curiosity, than I had observed in more southern districts; where the novelty of our appearance, from our long residence in the country, had lost much of its charms. In the course of our present march the people assembled in crowds, and hailed us with shouts of joy, spoke much of the tyranny and oppression of the French army, and acquainted us with many anecdotes respecting the enemy, which evinced the total disregard of the latter of every moral feeling and principle.

We have perceived a very sensible alteration in the climate, during our advance from Salamanca to this place; and have uniformly observed, that it approaches nearer to the standard of England in its usual degree of temperature than we could have previously supposed. When however the sun shines in its full force, the heat is certainly more intense than is usual in the hottest weather in England. The mountainous nature of the land, and its approximation to the Pyrenees and the sea, may account for the frequent alterations of temperature.

These sudden variations produce a very decided effect upon vegetation, particularly upon corn and vines, when contrasted with the same productions in the more southern parts.

Should Spain be finally liberated from the oppressors by whom she has lately been visited, (of which I indeed entertain very little doubt,) the people in the northern provinces, who are by no means slothful and disinclined to industry, may soon recover from the heavy losses they have sustained; for this part of the country, like many of the other portions of Spain, enjoys great facility of communication with the sea, together with a variety of advantages peculiar to the nation at large.

Upon the 15th of June we crossed the Ebro, and at the pass of San Martino entered what Buonaparte's aggrandizing system chose to hold out as annexed for ever to France, thereby rendering this river, instead of the Pyrenees, the boundary between the two countries.

There is something so striking in this pass, that I must endeavour to give you an account of it; though I sincerely regret my want of graphic power to furnish you with a drawing, in addition to the very imperfect notion which language can convey of its singularity and sublimity. After a long and fatiguing march, through a barren, rocky, and uninteresting country, over a rough stony road, from the early part of the morning till late in the evening, we arrived at the edge of a tremendous precipice, extending right and left beyond the reach of sight; and which rising a little as you advance, prevents the deep and wide chasm through which the river flows from being seen, till you come immediately upon it; when a prospect suddenly bursts upon the view of the most rich and interesting description that can be conceived, and additionally heightened from its contrast to the dreary region we had recently traversed.

The Ebro is here very narrow though deep, and meanders in a serpentine form through fertile values of corn and meadow-land, occasionally intermixed with numerous woods and villages; while each side is flanked by stupendous chains of mountains, partly rocky and barren, and partly cultivated, and affording walks for sheep and goats, which brouse upon their steepest summits. A few leagues up the country northward, towards the source of this river, many of the loftiest rocks rise perpendicularly one above the other, forming deep and extensive ravines, and some stupendous cataracts; creating altogether an assemblage of grand and sublime scenery, probably not surpassed in another part of the globe.

Two divisions of the army crossed the Ebro at this place; where the difficulties to be overcome, in traversing the steep descents, before you arrive at the paths which wind down the side of the mountain, (being very rugged, steep, and narrow,) prevented more than one horse or mule to pass at a time; and the artillery in particular, finding the obstacles so very difficult to surmount, delayed the progress of the baggage, and occasioned it to be late before it arrived in the field where we were bivouacked, the village of San Martino being too small to hold us. As we marched at three the following morning, several officers did not get their baggage long before it was time to repack it, which produced much inconvenience and some confusion.

Our march from the left bank of the Ebro was more unpleasant (nay even dangerous for cavalry) than our approach to it on the opposite side; but as no limbs were broken, what was suffered on the occasion was amply compensated by the novel and interesting scenery, of which in consequence we became spectators. Throughout the whole, indeed, of this part of our march it appeared as if we were traversing the very land of romance; extensive ravines every where intersect this mountainous country; while the summits of the mountains themselves rear their barren and rocky heads to the clouds, where they attract vast masses of snow, which at certain seasons, when melted by the sun, flow in torrents down the rock forming cataracts, and swelling the rivers into which they fall.

This wild and romantic scenery is pleasingly intermingled with rich corn fields, vineyards, olive-groves, and a few woods; among which the Ebro irregularly winds its majestic course through some of the finest parts of Spain, and passing by Saragossa, empties itself into the Mediterranean at a small distance below Tortosa.

The same species of country, as that which I have been describing, exists, though of a somewhat less striking description with respect to the mountains and ravines, during the whole route to this place. All things considered, the north-eastern part of the country forms the most interesting I have yet seen; though much of this interest may be derived from the circumstance of my not having hitherto met with any sufficient description of it.

Travelling about these parts cannot fail to afford a great deal of amusement, notwithstanding the dangers by which it might be attended to the solitary visitor of these almost unexplored regions. The whole of the country indeed wears an aspect of savage loneliness, which might justly excite apprehension in the boldest breast of robbery and assassination; particularly among a people so notoriously given to depredations and atrocities of this description.

I observed in several places the usual signal indicating the commission of a murder; which consists in a cross stuck into the earth, furnished with a painting representing the final state of retribution to which all earthly criminals are brought.

My attention has recently been entirely diverted from reflecting upon this interesting country, by the sudden, unexpected, and most glorious events of the 21st.

When we were about seven leagues from Vitoria, it was far removed from our contemplation that such important matters were in agitation, as we subsequently found had been actually accomplished; nor was it known even that any serious engagement was likely to take place, till we were far advanced upon our march. The commencement of firing of cannon and musquetry first instructed us with what was going on, and very shortly afterwards we arrived in the field of battle.

The bustle of a decisive action between two such powerful contending armies formed a novel and interesting scene to me, of which no time can obliterate the remembrance.

To my mind, unaccustomed to view things in a military point of view, the complete scene of confusion which took place in the evening, arising from the total rout of the enemy, who fled in all directions, leaving the plains strewed with every material which you may suppose a large army might possess, formed the most prominent part of the scene. The whole of the plains upon which the army moved were intersected by broad and deep dykes, where many an unfortunate soldier, and hundreds of horses and mules were lost in the general confusion.

In consequence of an action of this magnitude, a scene of plunder soon commenced, and was carried on in the manner usually attending such circumstances; while the abundant supplies of various liquors, bread &c. which covered the ground, enabled the men to regale themselves copiously, and furnished additional temptations to many irregularities incidental to similar situations; the whole view presenting the appearance of a great fair, or public rejoicing, intermingled with scenes of distress which may be better conceived than described.

With the general result of this decisive and distinguished action you must be already acquainted, and I have nothing to add to what you will learn from the public papers.

Of the town of Vitoria I hope to be able hereafter to give you some information; at present every thing is in such a state of confusion, that it is impossible to attempt a description of the place, or the events which have passed. Our late successes were the more extraordinary, because the enemy, from their occupation of Vitoria, possessed advantages which were not easily to be overcome.

A number of the inhabitants of the town are said to have followed the fortunes of Joseph, rather stay to witness the triumph of the English, and many of their own countrymen. It is affirmed also, that Joseph Buonaparte, before the engagement, made so light of the matter, that he persuaded numbers of the citizens to accompany him to the field of battle, in order to see how he would beat the English.

These followers, however, upon getting an insight into the real state of things, soon left him and his army, as it may be readily supposed, to their fate; though not without some individuals meeting with the natural consequences of the erroneous prophecies of their favourite.

I write this under canvass, in the woods, near to the small town of Salvatierra, and from which I dare not at present venture out, as it rains excessively, and the ground is knee deep in mud. Fortunately yesterday (the day of the battle) was very fine; but such weather as we have experienced on the present day, would have rendered lying out at night upon the open ground extremely disagreeable and distressing.

Where my next letter will be dated from is very uncertain but you may rest assured that I shall take the first opportunity of continuing my narrative.

After the Battle

Logrono, July, 1813. We have been proceeding over hill and dale with portions of the army, following different divisions of the enemy, till it has been at last found that cavalry are no longer necessary to the pursuit; and we have accordingly been ordered to this town, stationed upon the river bank of the Ebro, within about nineteen leagues of Pamplona, and twelve of Vitoria.

During the wet weather, when I last wrote, we were ordered into the town of Salvatierra for a few days; and I was there told, that Joseph Buonaparte had passed through the town, in his precipitate flight from Vitoria, with nothing about him except what he carried upon his back, the whole of his royal paraphernalia &c. being plundered; and after an hasty refreshment, accompanied by reported atrocities upon which I shall not enter, departed for France. From Salvatierra we advanced to Penacerrada, which formed a long march, occupying the whole day, from six in the morning till half-past nine at night; when, from want of accommodation in the town, we found a very comfortable bivouac in the midst of a fine wood, situated in a beautiful meadow. In the course of our route we marched through Vitoria; where the subsequent confusion, necessarily attendant upon the late action, was gradually giving way to that order and regularity which the change of circumstances naturally introduced. The majority of the wounded were brought in, and crowded in convents converted into hospitals for the occasion. The inhabitants and soldiery had been assiduously engaged in burying the killed, and removing the dead horses and mules. The cannon, tumbrils, and various carriages taken in the battle were collected together, and formed an immense mass of trophies wrested from the enemy. The greater part of the lighter and more moveable articles, money &c. having, as I understand, been plundered in a most irregular and shameless manner.

My stay at this place was necessarily short, so that I had no time to go about the town, or to visit its principal places. I could stay no longer a period than was requisite to procure a *déjeûné* at a *posada*, or eating-house; where the people, somewhat resembling the ass in the fable, showed an utter indifference as to which side they espoused, provided they had the furnishing of either with the articles of which they stood in need.

Many of the French, connected by intermarriages with the inhabitants, and other ties, still remain in the town.

The general appearance of the place is very respectable, and partakes more of comfort and affluence, than any I have seen since I left Salamanca. A very lofty chain of mountains intersects the country, from east to west, between Vitoria and the place from which I am now writing. We ascended this chain in the evening from the neighbourhood of Penacerrada. The road is wide and very smooth, and winds circuitously along the side of the mountains, for three or four miles, among ravines and woods of a very picturesque character. While we were traversing these regions a thick fog enveloped the surrounding heights, their tops being lost among the clouds, and over which we occasionally passed in partial obscurity; until gaining the summit, and descending into the plains below, an extent of country, further than the eye could reach, burst suddenly upon the view; the sun shining in the utmost splendor upon the expansive valley stretched before us; and interspersed throughout with fertile corn-fields, vineyards, and olive-groves the Ebro running through the whole district in a winding direction, bordered by flourishing villages on every side; among which latter about three leagues from Logrono, a neat and compact town stands upon an eminence, called La Guardia; which formed our head-quarters for the night, after crossing the chain of mountains I have just described, and where the novelty of our appearance, coupled with the late successes insured us much attention, civility, and respect. The road is here a *camino real* which is throughout in a generally good condition, with some few exceptions. These royal roads are usually constructed upon an elevated ground, probably after the Roman fashion, and are banked upon each side with a strong wall flush with the surface of the road.

On our way hither we have occasioned great curiosity and admiration, as the people assembled in crowds at the entrance of every town and village through which we passed, to hail our approach with the most extravagant demonstrations of joy, seeming satisfied, from the appearance and strength of our forces, that they were completely emancipated from the French yoke. The inhabitants of the town in which I write were resolved to lose no time in proclaiming the change of affairs, although it was humanely suggested to them, that, in case of the French returning, every one of them would be oppressed, or hanged, who assisted in the ceremony; yet they insisted upon proclaiming Ferdinand VII immediately; and he was accordingly reinstated upon his throne by proxy, the ceremony being attended by the civil authorities of the place, who formed a procession, escorted by our troops, to conduct his representative to a stage erected for the occasion in the market-place. In the evening the town was illuminated, and fire-works were let off, and the day following was to have been dedicated to bull-fights, and other civic rejoicings. In the former representation, however, an immense concourse of spectators was disappointed, by the bulls running away just previously to the period at which they were wanted, nor could they be induced to return by any endeavours of the peasants to bring them back; and the proposed festivities ended in a crowd of shouting vagabonds hunting some poor miserable scared bullocks about the ring, who very prudently preferred decamping to the celebration of the deliverance of the country.

Logrono is a populous and tolerably fine town, the streets are for the most part narrow, but well lighted and paved, and the houses in general are good. The Ebro flows by the north side of the town, and is here very shallow, and forms a few small falls at intervals. An handsome bridge, with a gateway in its centre, is thrown over the river at the northern entrance of the town, and a wide and open space is allotted for the market, which is generally well supplied, and particularly so with fruits of various kinds. British goods are here exposed for sale, the communication with Bilboa and other parts whence these things are imported, being well established. A gravel walk, walled round, nearly encircles the town, and a square on its southern side is well planted with trees, and abounds with promenades formed in different directions, and amply furnished with garden seats. These walks afford an agreeable rendezvous, when the weather proves favourable, for the higher classes; who, under other circumstances, usually frequent a long row of piazzas, called the Portalis, where the principal shops are found. A large convent in ruins supplies the place of barracks, and attached to it is a crescent forming a convenient parade, the enclosed space of which having been originally designed for bull-fights. A neat small theatre has been erected on this spot, at which a company of comedians and dancers occasionally perform.

The French, during their stay in this town, constructed a very spacious and convenient building for a military hospital, well furnished with a kitchen, laboratory, store-rooms, surgery &c. and on taking their leave left most of the furniture, such as bedding &c. behind them, which has proved a valuable acquisition to the Spanish army and ourselves. The town contains several handsome churches, the collegiate church in particular being a very elegant building, and well adorned on the inside with paintings, and other usual decorations common to a Spanish church, and it possesses a fine toned organ and a good choir of singers. The town is very well supplied with water from a copious fountain, that is constantly surrounded by women, whose business it is to carry it to and fro in large pitchers, which they rest upon the head, and poise in so dextrous a manner, as to be able to walk with considerable rapidity through the streets without holding the vessel with either hand, placing it on a towel wound round their heads, in a manner that forms an hollow for the reception of the vessel. When carried empty the pitcher is placed upon its side in the same situation.

Notwithstanding the apparent satisfaction expressed at our arrival, it is very evident, that, during the five years in which the French occupied this town, they ingratiated themselves with some of the people, who, in spite of the tyranny practised towards many of their countrymen, experienced no peculiar personal inconvenience from the general oppression and exaction. I am inclined to believe indeed, that, many of them, while praising the English, are really expressing opinions very opposite from those which they entertain. Our arrival, however, certainly produced a great sensation among them, but time must show, should we stay here long, to what extent their sincerity reaches.

The inhabitants and the English have now begun to interchange civilities with each other, and balls and other parties have been mutually given and received. These entertainments, on their part, do not afford me any high idea of Spanish society. The men are for the most part vulgar, vehement and noisy, and the women deficient in delicacy and manners. Before a party has been long assembled cigars are introduced, the smoke of which fills the room and creates an odour, that, as you may easily suppose, is not very agreeable to those unaccustomed to such practices; to which may be added the constant effluvia proceeding alike from both sexes. I have not yet observed, that the Spaniards possess a greater degree of intelligence, or information than their despised neighbours the Portuguese, nor could I discover any really good grounds upon which they can rest their boasted superiority.

I believe that time is not likely easily to reconcile me to this nation. I wish however not to judge too hastily, although every day furnishes me with additional reasons for lamenting the present condition of Spain, when compared with the notions we have imbibed of this once distinguished country.

War in the Mountains

Logrono, August, 1813. Since my last letter we have undergone a precipitate march to the neighbourhood of Pamplona. Of the glorious and well-contested battles of the Pyrenees, you have of course ere this been made acquainted. When we arrived we found the armies engaged among the hills close to the town, to the relief of which Soult had hastened in the most rapid and determined manner; but, no doubt to the severe disappointment of his friends within the walls of Pamplona, as well as mortification to himself, was beaten off just when they must have indulged confident expectations of his success. The two armies lying opposite to each other, upon the heights, produced at night an interesting and awful effect, each line being distinctly marked by the lights of its respective encampments. In one point of view a striking difference was observable between the two armies, the lights of the enemy being weak and thinly scattered, while those of the English were vivid and numerous. Upon this occasion the baggage was left some time in the rear, and we were therefore compelled to pass the night upon the bare ground, on hills devoid of any species of shelter from the weather, which however fortunately proved favourable. We were less happy in the circumstances attending our supply of food, than even in our lodging; for though there were several small villages in the neighbourhood, most of the houses belonging to them were in a deserted and desolated state, and furnished no description of sustenance whatever. Yet our march through this mountainous country was not devoid of interest, and indeed possessed considerable charms from the great beauty of the scenery. I was one morning, during our progress among the mountains, fortunate enough, through the help of a glass, to get a tolerably distinct view of Marshal Soult, who was reconnoitring from a great elevation, attended by a retinue of between forty and fifty horsemen, consisting probably of his staff, orderlies &c. He appeared to be a very tall and stout man.—I rode over the ground after the last and most distinguished battle which occurred in these parts, and beheld with astonishment the great strength of the enemy's positions, and the almost insuperable difficulties which our army had to surmount during the course of these most arduous achievements. Innumerable dead bodies, in a state of partial putrefaction, lay in all directions, a prey to wolves and vultures.

We have lately been in what is esteemed the finest and most productive part of the north of Spain. It is said that Navarre is not exceeded in fertility by any province in the country, unless it be some one among those bordering upon the Mediterranean. Every article of food is more easily procured and at a cheaper rate than in any other I have past through. The town of Pamplona, the capital of Navarre, lies at the foot of the small Pyrenees, and in an extensive valley surrounded by chains of verdant hills; the mountains of the Pyrenees rising at a distance, and lifting their rocky heads to the clouds, and assuming a great variety of grotesque and fantastic shapes.

The greater part of the cavalry is cantoned in villages about this country, while the majority of the infantry has proceeded to Saint Sebastian, where the enemy still holds out in the most obstinate manner; the Spaniards being left in the mean while to watch the garrison of Pamplona, which occasionally makes sorties to procure forage, as well as for the purpose of covering the entrance of mules loaded with provisions for the supply of the town. He is however too closely watched to effect much in these attempts. I have ventured within about three quarters of a mile of the town, which appears to be large and handsome, and very strongly fortified. I trust I shall have an opportunity of seeing it more closely at a future period, when its present occupiers are tired of the confinement and privations they endure.

Corn, vines, and olive trees are very abundant in these parts; and numerous vegetables, such as cabbages (of a very superior flavor), small but very indifferent potatoes, a large species of carrot, tomatoes &c. are greatly cultivated, with all of which the markets are very regularly supplied. The country also abounds with wood, and numerous villages and small towns, tolerably peopled, are scattered throughout the district; more pasturage is likewise to be observed here, than in most other parts throughout the northern provinces of Spain. Butter and cheese can be procured in great plenty throughout the whole of Navarre, and of a better quality than in the adjacent districts. They are sometimes made from cow's milk, but more generally from that of the goat; in which latter case the butter generally imbibes an unpleasant flavor, that however by washing can be easily removed. The cheese is somewhat insipid and hard, and indeed greatly resembles that, for which Suffolk, and some other counties of England have long been celebrated.

The red wine which is produced in Navarre is esteemed the best in Spain, possessing the richest flavor, and being of a stronger quality than any other. If drank from the barrel, when about two years' old, it is often found to be an extremely grateful and generous wine, but the goat's and pig's-skins, in which it is conveyed from place to place, from the pitchy preparation with which the inner surfaces are lined, impart a disagreeable taste common to all Spanish wine. This fine province must nevertheless be at present in a very different state to that which it enjoyed some years past, as the presence of the French armies has reduced its resources and greatly impoverished the inhabitants. In this advanced state of the season, it being now about the middle of August, the corn wears a rich and beautiful appearance and promises an abundant harvest.

Nothing can show the slight advance, that this country has made in the arts of agriculture, in a stronger light, than the nation's still adopting the clumsy and primitive mode of beating out the corn, which we learn from the writings of Moses was in practice among the Jews, and other nations of antiquity, when the arts of husbandry were nearly in their infancy. A circular stage is raised above the level of the ground, supported by a frame of wooden planks, and horses or mules, harnessed to an heavy sledge, are employed to draw it briskly round the ring, the corn being strewed in layers, for the purpose of being beaten out by this species of rude machinery passing over it. Sometimes, a man holding the reins, stands in the sledge to drive it round and the children are allowed to amuse themselves by riding in it, in order to increase the pressure. When a certain portion of grain is thus forced out, it is passed through different sieves; the whole process is certainly slow and imperfect, and exposed to many inconveniencies, and occasionally to waste.

The principal object of curiosity in this neighbourhood, is a very large and handsome aqueduct, which is thrown across a wide valley between two chains of hill emerging from the base of one and passing directly to that of the other. I counted ninety-seven arches supporting the canal. The centre arch is about fifty feet high, and the rest gradually diminish in height to the right and left. This work forms a conspicuous and beautiful object in the midst of the surrounding and extensive valley.

At the end of about three weeks we returned to our former quarters by slower degrees than we advanced; where, a change in the municipality unfavourable to our cause having taken place, we were not received with any of those enthusiastic demonstrations of joy which announce an hearty welcome, but on the contrary, experienced a coolness and indifference on the part of the inhabitants, which convinced me that they were more rejoiced at our removal than gratified by our return; though we find, as usual, the feelings of the populace a good deal divided. Of course, a great number of persons must derive benefit from the presence of our troops, and it may easily be imagined what an influence this circumstance alone necessarily produces upon the interests and feelings of the townspeople. The disposition of this place seems to afford a tolerably fair specimen of the spirit of the nation at large, and of its feeling towards the liberators of their country. That there are many sincere and grateful friends to the English I have little doubt, though I am equally persuaded that the majority, in their hearts, from a variety of causes and prejudices, prefer the French.

The people indeed are obviously divided in their opinion, as petty disturbances and contentions are eternally occurring, both parties on these occasions reviling and accusing each other with the bitterest asperity.

Those who favoured the French with particular indications of friendship, during their residence among the Spaniards, are now taunted by their opponents with showing an equal predilection for the English; while others, who from the pride of national character discover a coolness towards the English, bordering upon sulkiness, are denounced as traitors and friends of the French. In Vitoria, and other towns, I have heard that the same spirit of contention prevails, which indicates by no means that universal concordance of opinion upon public events, that I had been led to expect before my arrival in the country.

I think that the experience we may gain of nation will every day add strength to these ideas; and very probably, when the great work of driving the French out of the country is completed, the nation will be torn by internal commotions, and look upon England with as jealous an eye, and afford her no better welcome, than usually falls to the lot of the unfortunate being who steps in to mediate between husband and wife. The time probably will not be long, before it will be fully seen how slight a value Spain will set upon her recent deliverance, and the small advantage she will derive from it. In the mean while I cannot but feel an interest in the cause, from the remembrance of the greatness of the kingdom as it existed in better days; of which, the sudden burst of patriotism, when the insolent pretensions of the enemy were first made known, seemed to indicate a speedy renewal.

The Portuguese are altogether unanimous in their gratitude for the great services rendered them by the British; but, if the Spaniards possess this feeling at all, they are for the most part backward in acknowledging it; and, with an arrogance and self-sufficiency, peculiar to the nation, attribute much of the merit of every achievement that has been accomplished, during the various campaigns in the peninsula, to themselves. This they seem to consider as indicating a proper sense of their own dignity and independence and one 'most excellent *Senor*'.compliments his most 'illustrious friend' upon the vast exploits of their brave and fine armies, and sums up the whole by wishing his excellency 'may live a thousand years'

Perhaps it might be carrying the matter too far to conclude by wishing you a similar blessing.

At Rest

Passages, October, 1813. Since my last letter, circumstances have obliged me to quit the army for a short time, and to take up my abode in this place. When I commenced my journey hither the vine harvest was just began, and the wine countries through which

I have passed presented every where an interesting and lively scene. All hands of both sexes were put in requisition upon this occasion. The vines are universally dwarfish in appearance, being cut down, and not suffered to grow much beyond the ordinary standard of a small gooseberry-tree. The purple is much more cultivated than the white grape, and their respective flavors vary greatly in excellence on different estates, though none, that I have hitherto met with, approach the richness of a well-ripened grape from our English hot-houses. A taller species, and one bearing what is called the Malaga grape, and growing as ours generally do, is frequently cultivated in gardens, with superior care to that which is employed upon the vines solely appropriated to the produce of wine. The fruit of the former require also more ripening than that of the latter, and when gathered is afterwards hung up to dry, and potted with sugar. This, and some other of the Spanish sweet-meats, are very fine, such as pears, green-gages, the magnum-bonum plum, apricots &c. all are preserved with large quantities of syrup, and are handed about with wine and biscuit when the people are assembled in the evening, or during a morning visit. As soon as the bunches of grapes destined for the making of wine are cut off from the vines, they are put into conical barrels, one of which, when filled, is placed upon each side of a mule, and thus transported to the place allotted for the pressing out of the juice. This last operation is not conducted in the most delicate manner, and indeed it requires no small share of philosophy to overcome the feeling of disgust naturally excited by the early part of the process it undergoes. The wine is usually kept three months before it is fit for use; at which period, though it has passed the different stages of fermenting and refining, it is still considered to be extremely new. A green bush, or a piece of red rag suspended over the door of an house, is the usual signal for the sale of wine; and I have always considered that the best criterion of its quality is the degree of crowding, riot, and confusion, observable among the peasantry surrounding the place.

Due notice of the opening of a wine-house is obliged to be sent to the *alcalde*, or chief magistrate of the town; when a deputation of civil authorities proceeds to the spot, carrying a silver cup, out of which they take the first taste of the wine, and according as they approve or condemn, the licence is granted or withheld. The nefarious practice of mixing new wine with old, and that of an indifferent quality with the wine of the best vintages, renders it very difficult to procure any that is tolerable; and the only chance of obtaining it in good order is, to make interest to have a barrel or skin filled in the cellar when the shop is first opened. The overflowings, which must necessarily take place from this retail mode of disposing of the liquor, are cast indiscriminately into the same butt whence it was originally taken, with the occasional addition of no small quantity of water, and is then again retailed; and, as this is a ceremony often repeated, the quality of the wine may be pretty easily conjectured with which the last customer is accommodated.

An old skin, well saturated with wine, does not always impart a very strong and disagreeable flavor to the liquor; but in general, and especially if the skin be new, the pitchy composition with which its inner side is lined, impregnates the wine with a most powerful and austere taste, common to the ordinary red wine of the country, usually known by the name of black-strap.

An agreeable white wine is made from the Malaga grape, which is sweet, stronger bodied, and altogether a cleaner wine than the generality; most of the common white wines being very light and acidulous.

I shall now proceed to give you a description of my route to this place. As I slept a night at Vitoria, I had an opportunity of seeing more of the town, and to greater advantage than when I last visited it, as order and regularity had been long re-established and the inhabitants had become reconciled to their visitors.

The town lies upon the side of a steep hill, and possesses extensive suburbs; it appears very populous, and seems, by the profusion of shops, to have a considerable share of trade. It is, I think, inferior to Salamanca, both with respect to size and every other particular, excepting the facility of procuring almost every article of life,—it enjoys a great advantage in the abundance of French goods which are exposed for sale and it is exceedingly well furnished with hotels, cafes &c.

A large and well-stocked market is held during the week days, but every thing supplied is exorbitantly dear: poultry, game &c. though of a very inferior quality, are disposed of at prices, to which even the dealers of Covent-Garden Market are entire strangers, and every species of wine, except that of the country, is nearly as dear as in England.

Most of the streets are flagged, and some are open and handsome, with many good houses.

The principal square is spacious, uniform, and elegant, and its piazzas form the usual promenade, when the weather does not permit the people of fashion to walk upon a fine stone-built terrace, fenced with handsome iron railings, which stands about the middle of the hill above the market place, defended to the north by a long row of lofty houses.

The house which Joseph Buonaparte was pleased to establish as his palace, is very large and handsome, and has some gardens attached to it. The churches and convents are splendidly ornamented, and much in the usual style. The *camino real* leading from the town is very good, and is flanked some way on both sides by rows of poplars.

A depôt for the commissariat and medical departments is established in this place, and numbers of sick and wounded officers crowd the town. The road above-mentioned, which leads from the eastern gate of the town, is for the most part straight, and in excellent order; though after the bad weather, and the passing of the army, it is at present in many parts much cut up.

The country through which this road takes its course abounds with small towns and villages. The land within a few miles of Vitoria is plain, and possesses a great deal of pasturage, though the road subsequently shapes its course through lofty mountains, which are rocky and barren at their summits, but about halfway down become convertible into arable land, or afford pasture for the herds. The quantity of snow, which during a great part of the year lies upon those mountains, is thought to enrich (he neighbouring soil, and adapt it to vegetation.

Vines are not much cultivated in this part of the province of Biscay, though corn (and Indian corn especially) abounds, while thick forests very generally clothe the sides of the mountains. The pumpkin and gore are frequently cultivated, of which much use is made in various articles of diet.

The size of this species of fruit is enormous. In the corner of a kitchen I one day observed a large pumpkin partially devoured, which the people of the house told me they had been in the habit of employing, for culinary purposes, during the space of two years.

The principal town on this road, after leaving Vitoria, is Tolosa, a large and populous place, lying in a very fine and picturesque country, very hilly and fertile, and furnished with abundance of wood. The streets, houses &c. are neither neat nor handsome, nor does the town possess any striking beauties.

Farm-houses and *quintas* (gentlemen's seats) are occasionally scattered through the country, but their style of building is very deficient both in taste and comfort.

In the towns and villages upon this road, there is much less appearance of cleanliness and neatness in the arrangements of the houses, than is to be noticed farther south. The houses are mostly old, and in bad repair; the windows, where any thing of the kind occurs, are for the most part broken; and the chambers are universally floored with wood, which affords shelter for all kinds of vermin, and does not offer that wholesome and cleanly appearance which the neat brick floors, I formerly noticed, produce.

The towns and villages, though impoverished and shabby in their appearance upon a close inspection, nevertheless, present, when cursorily viewed, a very respectable, and often a very handsome air, which is probably in a great measure to be attributed to the fertile, diversified, and frequently romantic scenery which surround them.

The whole of this part of the country is plentifully supplied with water; and as I passed along I noticed several fine falls, cascades &c.

The country people of this province appear to be generally more stout and athletic than those which I have hitherto seen. The women, like those of Wales and Cornwall, seldom wear either shoes or stockings; they differ also in their countenances, dress, and general appearance from the people of the other provinces, being fairer, and having a more florid colour; wearing longer waists, and their hair platted together behind, and hanging down in enormously thick and long tails. Many of them use felt hats, stuck perpendicularly upon the top of their heads, over high caps; but this addition is adopted on holidays only.

The language of this province which is called the Basqueueze, is very peculiar, and greatly differs from the Castilian, (which is generally considered the purest Spanish,) as well as from every other dialect. It is not universally spoken, even in Biscay, few beyond the lowest orders being found, who are not fully as well acquainted with the Castilian as the harsh and vulgar language of the Basques.

St. Sebastian

Passages, Nov. 1813. Since I have been stationed here, I have had perpetual cause to regret the loss of a very accurate thermometer, which I brought from England, and which I have not been able to replace, as those offered for sale in the Spanish shops are calculated to answer any end, except that of giving an accurate idea of the state of temperature. Under these circumstances, however, though I cannot enter into the minutiæ of degrees, my own feelings partake sufficiently of the properties of quicksilver to assure me that you are much mistaken if you fancy England the most changeable of climates. Notwithstanding it is now autumn, the weather has recently been much too hot to admit of exercise or exposure to the noon-day sun. While in this town, which lies between lofty hills, the heat has lately been suffocating; yet suddenly, from a degree of temperature equal to that which is experienced in the West Indies, we have suffered a transition to the bleakest gales of an English October, succeeded by uninterrupted rains, which have deluged the country, overflowed the banks of rivers, washed away bridges, and reduced the bye-roads and lanes to a state that we should at home fairly condemn as impassable; but which are nevertheless, from the necessities of war, rendered to a degree accessable. The want of a snug fire-place is at this period severely felt; the smoakey chimney-corners are very distinct from those of the English farmers' fire-side, being no way inviting; while the little, occasional deficiencies in the roof and floors, together with holes representing windows, render the houses somewhat too airy residences at this season of the year, however cool and refreshing they may prove during the heats of summer.

The weather just now having moderated, in spite of the terrible state of the bye-roads, and even parts of the royal roads, has enabled me to take frequent rides, and enjoy the surrounding beauties of the country, which are certainly very great. The leaves are beginning to decay and fall from the trees, but I can easily conceive how extremely fine this variegated and hilly country must be in summer, situated as it is so near to the sea, adorned with the finest woods, and every where displaying the highest cultivation. The lesser Pyrenees take their rise in this neighbourhood, and extend towards Pamplona, uniting with the larger chain which runs from the Bay of Biscay to the Mediterranean, and divides France from Spain.

These mountains are extremely verdant, and are covered in many places with wood of various descriptions; much game is frequently found upon them, and you would scarcely believe that hunting is even practised in this mountainous district; a peculiar breed of dogs, greatly resembling our terrier, being employed for this sport.

A few leagues from Tolosa, the royal road to France, by Yrun is quitted on the left, in order to get to Passages in a more commodious way; not that I think that any way can easily be worse, than what is called the road to Passages, for the last league, when the high water prevents your taking the advantage of passing by the river side.

The first view, on gaining the summit of the hill near Tolosa, is very striking and extensive, and commands a wide prospect both by sea and land.

The multitude of detached houses, (or quintas,) hamlets, and villages which abound in this neighbourhood, interspersed with much wood, and the undulating lines of verdant hills studded with corn fields, form altogether a very rich and picturesque scene.

St. Sebastian with its castle, and a lofty light-house overhanging the sea, add much to the general effect of the prospect. This town, which once formed one of the finest places of Spain, and which still bears evident marks of its former splendor, is about a league from Passages, and close to the sea. Though now in a dreadful state of ruin, you may still readily trace some of the streets; yet not above thirty inhabited houses have survived the late destructive siege. A sort of market is re-established, and some shops have very recently been opened.

The houses appear to have been in general large and handsome, and the streets, for the most part, of a good width and uniformly built. There are several churches and chapels adorned with elegant towers, the chief of which possesses a very handsome exterior form, but on the inside it is less beautiful.

The town stands in a very strong position, is well fortified all round, and two spacious gateways, approached by draw-bridges, form the entrances. Some outworks, under Lord Wellingtons direction, are at present erecting, which will render it a very formidable obstacle in the way of the enemy, should he ever attempt regaining his lost ground.

The castle, which is a low and awkward building, stands on the summit of a very high hill immediately over the sea, and commands an extensive prospect on every side.

During the siege, the glare of light occasioned by the burning of the town, produced, I am told, at night, a most awful and sublime appearance, still further increased by the tremendous explosions which were continually occurring.

The town of Passages is very singularly constructed, and is as detestable as it is peculiar. The sea flows through a defile of mountains, and forms a navigable river to a considerable extent inland, affording a very safe and convenient harbour for shipping, with which it is now exceedingly crowded. This, added to the perpetually bustling scene that is going on, from the town being the chief depot of the army, imparts an interest to the place, which, joined to the beauty of the surrounding country, compensates, in some degree, for the extreme wretchedness of it accommodations.

The whole of the town consists of two exceedingly narrow, dirty, and uneven streets, one of which lies on one side of the river, and the other on the opposite bank; the communication between the two being carried on solely by means of boats, rowed by a delicate class of females, whose education appears to be much upon a par with that renowned seminary in our own country, which has so long been justly celebrated for the excellence of its fish, fragrant air, urbanity of manners, and refined language.

These daughters of Neptune despise the effeminate custom of wearing shoes and stockings; and, from their shortened petticoat and sleeves, display a pair of bronzed legs and arms, which, in size and muscular strength, rival those of any boatman upon the Thames.

Added to the petticoat, that is some times an English blanket, (the curious workmanship of which excites their universal admiration), a coarse linen, or cloth jacket, and a black beaver hat stuck straight upon the top of the head, form usually the simple attire with which these fair navigators are clothed.

Some few of them can speak a little Castilian, but, when a slight difference of opinion exists among them, the orators prefer arguing in the true Basqueueze. An unlucky wight, whose bed-room haplessly overhangs the river, needs no alarum bell to insure his early waking, as he is usually, with the rising sun, edified by these syrens of the neighbourhood with a few salutary modulations, which would render the expedient of Ulysses not a little desirable.

The population of Passages, under present circumstances, almost exceeds its accommodation, arising from the fugitives of St. Sebastian having taken refuge here, in addition to its former inhabitants; and also, from the numerous officers of every department of the army, whose head-quarters are stationed in this place; to which may be added that host of harpies, called sutlers, (who appear to follow the army solely for the purpose of putting it in mind of its wants), together with merchants, and adventurers of all descriptions.

The houses on both sides of the water are universally very confined, though generally lofty, and crowded by different families occupying separate rooms and floors. Few tolerable accommodations are to be procured, and frequently none at all. The width from the river side to the foot of the hills will not admit of broader streets than at present exist, though I know of no reason why they should be almost impassable to any other description of passengers than pedestrians.

British goods of every description are profusely vended, at an immense price, in all parts of the town; and the natives seem most cordially to unite with the English, who have come hither for profit, in imposing to the greatest possible extent upon the officers and men of the army.

An excellent market is held twice a week, where game, poultry, meat, vegetables, fruits &c. are well supplied, but at such prices as can seldom admit of the two first articles being indulged in. What do you think of an hare for three dollars, and a lean tough old fowl for nine shillings; the worst tea, three dollars a pound; butter and cheese, three shillings and sixpence? and so on in proportion.

About three miles up the river, situated among the hills, stands the small town of Renteria, the receptacle for sick and wounded officers, with which it is at present greatly over-stocked; and, as they are still daily arriving from the Pyrenees, the accommodations, which they are obliged to put up with, are quite shocking to the feelings of humanity.

As I am about to return to my old quarters, through the province of Navarre by the Pamplona road, I must shorten this letter, and refer you to another for a description of every interesting particular which may occur.

Travelling

Pamplona, December, 1813. As the town of Pamplona is now in the possession of the allies, an opportunity has been afforded me of my curiosity in seeing the interior of this celebrated city; and the road through it being for the most part remarkably fine, and the journey somewhat shorter than by the way of Vitoria, induced me to give it a decided preference, which the result has amply compensated.

Travelling alone, in the very depth of winter, along a less populous and frequented road than usual, and through a mountainous country, together with the accounts of robbery and plunder in which all the natives agree, made me entertain some little fears for my own safety and that of my baggage. These reports however I find, on experience, to be greatly exaggerated; for the few people that I have met with upon the road behaved with marked civility and attention, nor did I perceive any grounds whatever for the cautions I had received.

That a disposition does exist, among some bravos and outlaws who infest the mountainous parts, to rob, plunder, and even assassinate, I have no doubt, though certainly not in the degree that has been represented. Deserters from the army form a considerable portion, I am told, of these marauders, and among them some, I am sorry to say, have been occasionally recognized as British subjects.

Upon the Bayonne road, as it winds through the mountains towards Yrun, many robberies have recently been committed, the place being, from its lonely situation, peculiarly exposed to attempts of this nature; while the neighbourhood of our army, on the opposite side of the Pyrenees, necessarily holds out a perpetual temptation to the plunderers who infest these defiles.

The usual mode of attack practised by these robbers, very much resembles the one employed in the following instance, which came almost immediately under my own knowledge. A person passing this road, and entering upon a solitary part of it, was suddenly arrested in his progress by two robbers, who at first suffered him to pass them a short distance unmolested, when one of them, in opprobrious language, commanded him to stop, at the same time making signs to him to let fall such valuables as he had about him, while his companion, presenting his piece, pretty forcibly seconded the demands of his associate. Unfortunately, the object of the attack paid little regard to strong admonition, and quietly continuing his route, received the contents of the musket in his arm, but being well mounted was fortunate enough to effect his escape.

As far as I have been able to discover, from conversing with the natives of this delightful province, they are unanimous is our favour, and by much the most determined people in the cause which I have met with in Spain. The English are held very high consideration among them, while the French, for tolerably substantial reasons, are equally detested. The animosity of the inhabitants towards the Portuguese is by no means of the acrimonious description which I have noticed in the other provinces of Spain, though I have no where remarked a cordial feeling between the two countries; although the Spaniards are assuredly under great obligations to the former nation, for the powerful co-operation of its army in their own country; while the Portuguese have nothing on their part to thank the Spaniards for, having on the contrary, much cause to be dissatisfied with the whole of their proceedings.

It has often vexed me to have repeatedly heard the Portuguese distinguished by the Spaniards by the appellation of the 'the bad nation', and without reason, condemned for cowardice and want of enthusiasm, charges which might have been more justly retorted upon themselves; and I have frequently noticed sneers and expressions of contempt fall from Spanish officers strongly indicative of hostility, when in the presence of Portuguese officers most highly distinguished for their conduct and gallantry; rendered doubly galling by the extravagant assumption of the Spaniards, when comparing themselves with the Portuguese.

These, and many other characteristic traits, will furnish a general idea of the disposition and temper of this nation, and shows the utter impossibility for the two countries heartily concurring in the common cause.

At Tolosa, the two great roads branch off, one for Vitoria through the province of Biscay, and the other by the way of Navarre to this town, the latter altogether extending to a distance often leagues.— Throughout this part of the country, the royal roads are all furnished with league stones, pointing out to travellers the exact distance from one place to the other, somewhat resembling the mile-stones in our own country, though of a much larger description.

Notwithstanding the Spanish leagues are shorter and more accurately laid down than those in Portugal, yet they are still far from being perfectly correct; as they are often measured by the people of the country, where no league-stones are to be found, by time, making an hour and a league synonimous terms; to which, as a farther inaccuracy, may be added, their being not unfrequently divided into large leagues, small leagues, and very short leagues, agreeably to the respective distances of the different towns and villages. I should, however, doubt whether the distance of any description of Spanish leagues, exceeds three miles; though it rarely happens, where there are no league-stones that any information can be relied upon from the computations of the common inhabitants of the country; for it is usual in collecting their different opinions to find they all disagree, and the casual enquiries upon the road serve only to puzzle and disappoint you.

The different halting-places upon the road, between Tolosa and this town, consist of very small and poor villages, which circumstance, to a solitary traveller, becomes of less importance than to a regiment on its march; for, it must be hard indeed, if a tolerable accommodation cannot be afforded a single person.

The civility and hospitable attentions which the inhabitants evinced, removed every unpleasant feeling that might have otherwise arisen from their very limited means of affording a comfortable reception.

A decent kitchen-fire, cheerful countenances, and a room capable of excluding the inclemencies of the season, may here be considered indeed as the most essential requisites; for you must remember that in our mode of travelling in this country, we carry certain articles and accommodation about us, which render other deficiencies of minor consideration; a practice which conveys an idea of wealth and independence, to those who have not seen much of the British army, very advantageous to our cause, and often affording no small share of amusement.

The curiosity of the inhabitants is strongly excited as each little article of the canteen is brought out, and their admiration at every contrivance belonging to the conduct of the baggage, resembles the effects produced upon savages when placed in a similar situation.

Populous as this province appears, the people, remote from the towns seem to be very little acquainted with the civilization of other European countries. Their mode of squatting themselves down in circles at their doors, their dress, or rather deficiencies of dress, their extreme ignorance and want of information, their manners and habits of life, partake more of the nature and disposition of the Moors, in the earlier and barbarous periods of their history than of those of any other nation.

Their daily diet consists generally of very simple materials, such as bread, cabbage, and some other vegetables, and herbs made into broth, roasted chesnuts &c. the latter forming, among those who are unable to afford a frequent indulgence in the luxuries of bread, meat, and vegetables, the chief means of subsistence. Their manner of cooking is extremely good. Small earthen pots, called by them pinellos, and filled with their provisions, are placed by the side of a wood fire to stew; and the advantage they possess over our metallic ones, is very conspicuous in the dressing of hashes, stews, soups &c.

As I was sitting with my patrone (the master of the house, who was a curate,) one evening, over a wood fire, in the kitchen, I observed a cauldron containing a vast quantity of chestnuts roasting, and I concluded from their quantity that they must be for sale. When sufficiently done, however, they were all thrown into an heap upon the floor, in the midst of a family circle huddled round the fire, consisting of women and children, (inmates of the house,) who in a short time cleared away the whole, each person finishing the supper with a draught of cold water. This food to a stomach accustomed to such kind of diet, no doubt proves nourishing, for the inhabitants of this province all look healthy and fresh-coloured, and appear to be active and industrious. It is generally noticed indeed that the women and children for the most part to the north-east of Spain possess fairer complexions, and more colour in their cheeks, together with stouter bodies, than any other inhabitants of the kingdom. The men who labour in the fields are as brown as their neighbours, but I think have usually the advantage in point of strength and athletic limbs. The extreme vicissitudes of heat and cold to which they are exposed, probably occasions this distinction, as the uniformly scorching heats of more southern parts seems to diminish the stature of the labourers.

The women, I observed, as I passed along, occasionally assist the men in the labours of the fields, which are upon this road dedicated chiefly to the cultivation of turnips, and, in some few instances, to corn and hemp. The mode of preparing the earth, when the harvest is over, for ensuing crops, is somewhat singular. Three or four men abreast, each furnished with a large iron triple fork, with a cross-bar, somewhat resembling our dung-fork, turn up the earth as they proceed over the field, by driving the instruments into it with the assistance of their feet, and then withdrawing them, performing each motion together in as exact unison as accompanies the manoeuvres of a well drilled file of soldiers; a woman follows with the seed, which she casts into the earth as fast as it is turned up, succeeded by another, whose employment consists in beating down the sod, and covering the grain. Here is evidently, speaking generally, a waste of manual labour, which might be saved by the simplest piece of machinery used in our own country, and the employment of mules or oxen requiring the attendance of one man only; though in many parts of Biscay and Navarre, where I have seen this method practised, it would be impossible to substitute a plough, from the nature of the country, as many of their cornfields lie on the side of mountains, so steep as to be inaccessible to mules and carriages of any kind. Generally speaking, however, nothing can show the very backward state of this country more fully, than such specimens as these of their absolute ignorance of one of the commonest and most important occupations of life. It may, notwithstanding, be a question whether the people would be benefitted, under present circumstances, by the introduction of the more perfect machinery commonly in use among our own agriculturists.

It now only remains for me to give you an account of this city before I resume my journey.

Pamplona is certainly, in every point of view, by far the best town I have seen either in Spain or Portugal, and possesses greater sources of comfort and amusement.

Its vicinity to France, and the sea-ports upon the coast of Biscay, which, from the excellence of the roads are easy of access even to carriages, combined with a ready communication with the metropolis, and the fine country of Catalonia and Saragossa, all render this place eligible as a residence for those engaged in the pursuit either of business or of pleasure.

The town itself is spacious, airy, and handsome, the streets wider than those of most other towns, and the houses are generally high, and contain numerous apartments, kept usually in very excellent order. The entrance to the city is noble, and as a completely fortified town has a more imposing coup-d'œil than Portsmouth.

Its elegant and lofty spires are seen from a great distance, which, together with its walls, bastions, and turrets, give it an appearance of great strength and grandeur. The northern part of the town is much elevated, while the other quarters of it are nearly level with the land mound; the meanderings of the Ebro are seen approaching the north end of the town from a considerable distance, and, after sweeping the foot of the walls, glide off to the southward.

An handsome bridge is thrown over the river, which conducts you In die place through a spacious gateway, and by a draw bridge, where captain's guard is stationed with very strict orders relative to the admission of strangers. A portion of the hussar brigade has recently been quartered line, but at present it is entirely a Spanish garrison. Several quintas and small rows of houses in the suburbs are scattered upon the banks of the river near the town, but the French have done them considerable injury; while within the town they appear to have confined their cupidity to the plundering only of every private house in the city.

In the centre of the town, stands a large and usually crowded marketplace, very abundantly, but not cheaply supplied, and containing an handsome municipal-house, adjacent to which lies a very spacious square with piazzas around the greater part of it. One side of the square is adorned by row of elegant white stone houses though the other sides are extremely deficient in uniformity, and beauty of appearance.

The theatre is a small and dirty building, and its arrangements are somewhat curious. Besides the pit, which consists of little boxes, each capable of holding one person only, and numbered to correspond with the ticket of admission, are three rows of galleries, where nothing but standing room is allowed the audience, there being no seats; with the exception of a few chairs in the centre row, where the higher classes of ladies sit, and the official dignitaries of the town, who are in a separate portion of the circle, and parted from the rest. The lower circle admits the *profanum vulgum*, and the upper, the intermediate class, while the generality of gentlemen sit in the pit; though in all parts of the house the men are separated from the women. I observed a sufficient force of grenadiers, stationed in different parts of the house to take all the assembly, if requisite; and they enforced silence most rigourously, and with an air of authority, which I perceived, in many instances, was very offensive to some of the audience, who had occasionally trespassed by holding a conversation too loud for these mighty warriors to endure. There are a number of gambling-tables, posadas or eating houses &c. where the people generally spend their evenings. Many public buildings are interspersed about the town, hospitals, and other charitable endowments, convents &c. some of which are very handsome, spacious, and costly. The churches are generally very old and shabby in appearance, with the exception of the collegiate church, which is a very large and handsome building, standing upon the top of an hill, at the northernmost end of the town, in the centre of a paved square, surrounded by iron railing. It appears very ancient, and of completely gothic architecture, decorated as is not uncommon with gothic edifices, by curious figures representing monkies, pigs, dogs &c. in various uncouth attitudes. The front has been modernized, and is very finely ornamented with carvings of scriptural stories, and the portico is supported by plain massy pillars.

A royal palace, built in former days, still exists, but it is more remarkable for its antiquity than its beauty.

The next building of consequence is the citadel, at the southern side of the town. It occupies a large space of ground, and consists chiefly of a crescent of small houses, where the artificers &c. reside: it has no tower, or any thing indicating a castellated appearance above its walls. A walk round the ramparts, by a broad gravelled road, which encircles the town, commands many fine views of the surrounding country.

The fortifications are unusually strong, and doubly ditched, and are much frequented by the people of the town.

Interposed between these works and the city, on one side, a large square, well gravelled, ornamented with fine poplar trees, and furnished with seats for the company (resembling those in St. James's Park) forms a parade for the exercise of the troops, and for the inhabitants to promenade in.

The town, though still populous, is reduced of late years to a smaller number of inhabitants than it formerly possessed, and these are much impoverished from their late connexion with the French. As they make their fires with wood only, they suffer grievously from the high price it bears, and the great deficiency of it in the neighbourhood. Owing to this scarcity, and their being obliged to obtain fire-wood from a considerable distance, they have a method which lessens the expense that would otherwise be attendant upon land carriage. Contractors supply the town from the woods of the adjacent mountains, by means of the river, into which logs are thrown that float down a certain way, when their course is turned by a framework across the river into a small canal, which empties itself into a lake, where the wood is collected together, and sold to the people.

The government of this town possesses a more extended jurisdiction than that of most others in Spain, and consists of a governor, teniente, (king's lieutenant) with an alcalde, and the usual inferior train of officers.

The dialect of the inhabitants appears to border a good deal upon the Basqueueze, with a considerable portion of the dialect of the province. In other parts of Navarre, they mingle their dialect still more with that of Biscay.

Life & Death

Logrono, February, 1814. After encountering bad roads and severe weather, in retracing my steps from Pamplona to this place, I have once more taken up my quarters in Logrono. The principal places upon the route hither are tolerably good, for Spanish country towns, and the comforts and civilities I received from the inhabitants, upon whom I was quartered, compensated for the miseries of travelling slowly through a part of the country, which, though very fine in fair weather, must of course, lose a large portion of its attraction from the severity of the season at this period of the year. The first town which I stopped at, in my road to this place, Puente la Reyna, is very neat and populous, pleasantly situated on the banks of the Ebro, and surrounded by beautiful and picturesque scenery.

This town is remarkable for the best Navarre wine, which is superior in flavor and quality to that of any other produced throughout the country, and is to be purchased at a very reasonable price.

Estella, which forms the next stage, is also a very respectable town; and Los Arcos, though less than either of the former, possesses many advantages which entitle it to attention: between the latter and Logrono, upon a very high hill, stands the small and agreeable town of Viana, the principal church of which is a very handsome building, and throughout is very elaborately decorated. The inhabitants of all these towns are in better circumstances than the generality of those in the neighbouring district, and they uniformly evince very great friendship and hospitality towards the English.

The disposition to faction, and party spirit, seems to be gathering strength in Logrono; and it appears, that those who support the established abuses of the Spanish government have pretty just reason for supposing, that, on our departure, they will become the victims of the inherent bigotry, which, I am sorry to say, appears generally to pervade the majority of the Spanish nation; it not being unusual for mobs to collect in the streets denouncing those as traitors who are favourable to our cause.

Among the parties chiefly marked out for persecution is the body of the clergy at large, all of whom, from self-interested motives, and an adherence to the stronger side, are of course devoted to our cause. The peasants and labourers, emancipated from the tyrannical laws of their old government, and the terrors of the inquisition, naturally give their opinions with a degree of violence proportioned to the restraint under which they had so long suffered, and with a confidence, which in former days would have subjected them to the most dreadful ecclesiastical visitations. Their proceedings, as you may well suppose, are very galling to the priests, who, being anxious to restore their former power, take part with one side or the other, according as either may possess the greater preponderance to enforce their pretensions.

It is, however, most sincerely to be hoped, for the interests of humanity, that the dangers attendant upon priestcraft are not likely to take place again very speedily; and that the inquisition, so repugnant to the best feelings of human nature, and so subversive of all social enjoyments, is now permanently abolished. If ever their exiled monarch be permitted to revisit his native land, it is natural to suppose, and sincerely to be desired, that he will have learnt in the school of adversity, to which he has been exposed, a degree of liberality, sufficient to induce him to act upon somewhat more lenient and enlightened principles, than those which he might have been inclined to adopt, before disappointment and misfortune had opened his mind to the strong and indefensible rights of man.—Should the priests, instead of their former violent and intolerant behaviour, be led from the circumstances of the times, to pursue a different line of conduct from that which they have been accustomed to follow; and, like their great master, consider humility and forbearance as a better means of subduing the passions of men, than violence and torture, in all probability they will soon reap the benefits which are ever attendant on reason and moderation, not only in regard to individual advantage, but also to that of the nation at large. Were it possible, from what has recently occurred, to produce any thing like a system of this nature, Spain would have no reason to regret the sacrifices she has made, nor the dreadful loss of blood and treasure which she has expended, during the late perilous struggle. She has been, indeed, plunged deeply in wretchedness, but it has taught her, or ought to have done so, a valuable lesson, from which she will in all probability, derive great ultimate benefit.

I have occasionally given you some anecdotes respecting the extent to which the craftiness of the priests is carried, in maintaining the great weight, authority, and influence they possess over the minds of the ignorant and bigotted people; and of which perhaps, the following fact, which occurred to one of the principal inhabitants of this town, furnishes a striking example. An individual, possessing a large fortune, and some consideration in the place, and, who had in consequence, been very closely and piously attended by every description of religious orders; and who, according to the usual custom, had rested the salvation of his soul upon the opinions of ecclesiastics, bequeathed a coach to the church, adapted for the sole purpose of carrying the host, religiously styled the carriage of God; upon the pannels of which are displayed a representation of the Deity, the heavens, angels &c. None but a priest dare sit in this carriage, and the man who drives it is bare-headed in all states of the weather; while the family to which it belongs pride themselves extremely upon this sacred vehicle, every member of which is, in consequence, considered as possessing great claims to piety in the estimation of the community.

Another instance of devotion and enthusiasm I shall now mention, which actually happened in this place, and which, occurring from the same spirit, might have produced effects of a very tragical nature.—A solemn mass was performed for the repose of the souls of those heroes who had fallen in battle. An altar was raised in the aisle of the church, adorned with funeral and warlike trophies, and a quantity of swords were suspended round it. In the evening of the day of the ceremony, a mob collected, and repaired to the house of the Spanish commandant, entreating his permission to gratify the holy and loyal zeal with which it was animated, by rushing to the church, seizing the arms which rested upon the altar, and plunging them into the bosoms of every one whom they chose to deem a traitor to the cause. The pusilanimity of the commandant had nearly caused this barbarous project to be executed literally. But the timely interference of the more reflecting, and better-disposed part of the citizens, prevented the horrible carnage that might otherwise have ensued.

Stationed as I am, at one place, and very likely to remain so for some lime longer, I shall take up the various circumstances which are daily occurring, without any particular regard to the order in which they present themselves.

A few days ago, I was at a Spanish christening, which of all the church ceremonies that I have witnessed, is assuredly, the most absurd and ridiculous. The infant is so hauled and pulled about that it really seems to be in danger of suffocation, not to mention the extreme risk it incurs of being poisoned or drowned. The family party goes to the church dressed very finely, and the child is decked from top to toe with every description of finery, though judging from what I have witnessed, the unfortunate sufferer does not seem greatly to enjoy its "vests and tunics." Crosses are marked with sweet-oil upon its neck and face, and salt is put into its ears and mouth; the greater part of its clothes are then removed, and a large chalice of cold water is soused upon its head, which is held over the font; ceremonies, which, as you may easily imagine, the devoted little creature combats to the utmost of its faculties, making the most outrageous squalling, till the miseries it endures absolutely deprive it of the power of farther resistance. After undergoing a change in its dress, it is made to hold a wax taper, about five feet in height, to a painting of the Virgin; which ceremony being over, a kind of jig is played upon the organ, in honor of the new-made Christian. The friends then depart, casting copper pieces among the crowd of boys assembled round the church door to await the expected scramble.

The ceremonies of burial differ materially from ours, and are not wholly devoid of solemnity, of which, however, the many instances of superstition accompanying them greatly diminish the force. A procession (and nothing can be done without one) goes from the church, attended by priests in their robes, and a train of assistants carrying large lights, banners, paintings, crosses &c. suitable to the occasion, and chanting as they pass along to the house of the deceased. The body is thence carried to the church, where a requiem is performed over it, and it is then interred.

The funeral of a rich man is very splendid, and attended by a larger concourse of people than is usual among the lower classes. The relations and friends of the deceased do not attend, though in some instances, where more state is observed, the domestics join the procession, in which case they are dressed in their best liveries, and carry large lighted candles in their hands.

The Spaniards have a disgusting custom, when a poor person dies who cannot afford to pay the expences of a funeral, of exposing the body at the door of an house, and a plate is placed upon its breast, to receive the contributions of the passengers, to defray the charges of burial.

The priests and others, who are in daily terror of popular commotions, have been long dreading the carnival; which, however, has passed off without any violence being offered them; though some of their windows have suffered, and a few of the more unpopular have had the alarming satisfaction of seeing themselves represented dangling from a gallows upon the walls, or burning in effigy opposite their windows. The carnival has lasted three days, and the great concourse of people which thronged the streets was kept in awe by a party of the Spanish foot-guards, that marched into the town for the purpose. Pantomimes and processions, illustrative of the times, furnished the chief morning amusements, and fire-works and illuminations those of the night. A figure of Buonaparte was carried about, striding a large globe, which was afterwards burnt with great eclát. The populace, during these festivities, took occasion to pass a singular piece of justice and slur upon the priests, which no doubt caused the latter to lament very feelingly the loss of the Inquisition. Men dressed in the garb of the curas, ornamented with horns and feet resembling those with which Satan is usually depicted, pranced about the streets in all directions, with vases of incense burning in their hands. A second effigy of Buonaparte was placed in a chair upon an high pole; and another of King Ferdinand sat in a neighbouring balcony, supported by the British lion upon his right, which, at a given signal, was moved forwards upon a line to the tip of one of Buonaparte's boots, spitting fire from its nostrils, and communicating with the figure exploded a variety of fire-works, each leg and arm being blown off separately, till at length the whole of the body, chair, and the various paraphernalia were destroyed, to the great admiration of the populace. Among the various amusements of the carnival, one of the most frequent pleasantries in which the Spaniards delight to indulge themselves, is throwing handfuls of flour about at each other, and filling their mouths with water, in order to spit it into the faces of the by-standers. This joke, though apparently much relished by the natives, did not appear to be equally so by their English friends. The playing the *hohlee*, an entertainment among the Marhattas, which I have seen described in a work recently published relative to that people, seems to bear a great resemblance to this custom; though the latter nation, on these occasions, employing syringes instead of their mouths, renders the game more decent and less objectionable; particularly when we consider, that from the habits of the Spaniards, the water which they spout forth must be pretty highly flavored with garlic, and other fragrant odours.

A few days after the intelligence arrived of the liberation of Ferdinand, which excited great commotion among the people, the town was again Illuminated, and fire-works displayed, while the effigy of the King was drawn about the streets, seated in a phaeton, and attended by a band of music and a guard of honor.

A short time will show whether the conduct of Ferdinand will justify those rejoicings; for my own part I fear, that, like most other monarchs placed under his peculiar circumstances, he is more likely to recollect what he has been, than derive any advantage from the hard, though unpalatable lessons which misfortune might have taught more humble individuals; for, from what I have heard of his character, I greatly apprehend that he is likely to be guided in his future government by the direction of the priests, and those who are interested in suppressing that spirit of liberty and information, which, from a variety of causes has lately been engendered among the people.

I must now begin to think of closing my remarks upon this country, as we are about to enter France; and for many reasons that will be obvious to you, I hope I am not likely to visit it again, at least not till the country is placed under more auspicious circumstances. I must, however, while I condemn the Spaniards, not be understood to apply my censure universally. The fairer half of the nation certainly claims exemption; for, with a little polish from more refined education than is at present within their reach, I cannot conceive (from the little observation I have been able to make among the better classes,) a more agreeable, fascinating, and beautiful race of females. They appear to me to differ very little from the Portuguese women in any respect, and if a distinction exists, the superiority rests with the former. Their dress is becoming and simple, consisting principally of the black gowns and lace mantillas worn by the Portuguese ladies. In their disposition they are by no means inclined to distance and reserve. On the contrary, their principal failing consists in a species of lightness and coquettishness of manner; which, in their intercourse with the English, often affords but too solid grounds for those feelings of suspicion and jealousy inherent in the Spanish character.

Into Napoleon's Country

St. Jean de Luz, March, 1814. Though I am now breathing French air, I do not perceive that gay and lively effect which is so generally ascribed to it; but I am determined not to be disappointed, for notwithstanding appearances are somewhat unfavourable at present, they will most probably mend; as any considerable change in these respects cannot now be fairly expected, from the extreme wetness of the weather, accompanied by cold and violent March winds, together with heavy roads, and all the train of evils attendant upon the breaking up of a severe winter; while the long presence of two powerful contending armies has by no means tended to diminish those inconveniencies. On the 18th of March we quitted Logrono, to the great sorrow, I believe, of a few of the inhabitants, who, from our long residence among them, felt a certain degree of interest in the prolongation of our stay; though with respect to the generality, I have reason to believe that the satisfaction of parting scene was nearly reciprocal. In the first instance we followed the route through Vitoria, by Briones, Aro, and La Puebla; and from the former town we pursued the *camino real à Francia*, or high road to Bayonne. To Vitoria the road was new to me, never having before traversed that part of the country. The scenery during this portion of our route was for the most part exceedingly picturesque, and, though mountainous, very fertile and woody, while the Ebro meandered through the vallies in a very interesting and beautiful manner. The heights of

La Puebla, celebrated from the circumstances of the glorious 21st of June, appeared at a distance, crowned with snow. Vines and olive-trees were found in greater abundance than in any other part of the country through which we have passed. Briones is a neat, pretty little town, built on the summit of an high hill, with suburbs extending below it, and though its streets are narrow, they are nevertheless clean, and furnished with good houses. An open space is left in the centre of the town where the best are situated, and it commands a fine and extensive prospect. Were it possible to combine the comforts and refinements of England with the natural advantages of the north-eastern provinces of Spain, they would form the most enchanting country to inhabit which I can conceive; but, the manners and customs of the Spaniards, the wretched state of society, and their ignorance and bigotry, combine to render at once, what would otherwise ensure a large proportion of enjoyment, a subject merely for passing admiration and lasting regret.

The climate is of all others the most genial, being less variable than that of England, yet, by no means monotonous, equally removed from the intense extremes of more northern and southern latitudes. In this delightful region, the sportsman may find abundant sources of health and amusement, without incurring any of the dangerous risks arising from violent exercise and exposure in more hot and oppressive climates. Foxes, hares, partridges, wood cocks, snipes &c. are to be met with in great numbers.

The village of La Puebla is, in itself, small, and not attractive, but the neighbouring country is highly so, and very productive in corn, vines, olives &c. The latter are smaller, and less flavored than those grown in the southern provinces.—They are gathered in during the autumn, and form a portion of the Spanish diet, the oil expressed from them being the principal source of emolument to the proprietors of olive-groves. The superfluous branches of the trees, as well as those of vines &c. are burnt to a kind of charcoal, which is then chopped into small pieces, and sold under the name of tirso,[1] and being placed in a copper vessel, or brasero, is used for the warming of rooms, fire-places not being generally adopted in this or any other part of Spain.

Upon the road between Briones and La Puebla stands a very neat town called Aro, which we passed through without halting, and following our march from Vitoria, we pursued the Bayonne road already described in a former letter. The weather, at this period became cold and showery, as we approached the Pyrenees. From Alegria, a little dirty town, forming our last stage in Spain, we marched on to St. Jean de Luz, whence, not finding accommodations for the horses, we were obliged, though the night was dark and far advanced, to proceed a few miles farther to neighbouring villages, and midnight arrived before we could get billetted, after a long and tiresome journey of nearly fifty miles, through heavy roads and indifferent weather. Towards the latter part of the march, the weather however moderated, and enabled us the better to enjoy the fine scenery of the frontiers, and around the pass through the small Pyrenees.

The whole of the border country consists of one uninterrupted range of mountains, through which the Bayonne road is cut, and which, upon the Spanish side, is in very bad order. The last town, on the right bank of the Bidassoa, through which we passed, is Yrun, a small, dirty, and confined place. The houses, notwithstanding, are apparently comfortable, and their windows and doors in better condition than usual. The inhabitants are composed of a pretty equal mixture of French and Spanish.

After gaining the summit of the hills through the pass, an extensive prospect presents itself of a large portion of the coast of both countries; in which the mouths of the Bidassoa river, with rich meadowlands upon the French side, and several small towns and villages, together with the ancient fortress of Fuenterrabia overhanging the sea, form the most distinguished features. This fortress is very strong, and its ramparts are surmounted by a lofty castle. One of the principal productions of this part of the country is cyder; and in consequence, extensive orchards, well-stocked with apple-trees, every where abound, among which, a dwarfish kind bears most prolifically, the fruit being of a ruddy colour, and is that which is chiefly used for the making of cyder.

After passing the bridge, recently erected for the passage of our troops, we arrived for the first time upon French ground, by the route of the Bayonne road; which runs over an hill from the left bank of the river, and commands an extensive and beautiful view of the sea and coast upon one side, and the great chain of the Pyrenees on the other. It being late in the evening when we entered France, the surrounding prospect was soon shut from our view.

Since we have been in this neighbourhood, the weather (usually wet in these mountainous regions) has afforded me but few opportunities of gratifying my curiosity, by observing the novel and interesting scenery around: I have, however, succeeded in one or two instances between the showers, in rambling about St. Jean de Luz and the adjacent hills. The former is, at this time, crowded to excess, from its being the headquarters of most of the staff, and the consequent resort of its innumerable followers. The place itself is extensive and very populous. The houses, in general, are of a mean size, with but very few exceptions; yet they, notwithstanding, excel most materially even those of more imposing Spanish towns, in the superior air of comfort and neatness which they possess. Windows with unbroken panes of glass, and furnished with proper shutters, and doors made air tight; together with a frequent custom of white-washing the walls of the houses, and painting the window-shutters and doors green, render them obviously preferable to the more lofty and spacious mansions of the Spaniards; who are, in general, strangers to the above comforts, and, with the vilest taste, paint the walls of their houses, doors &c. with hideous and fantastic designs, in ill-combined and glaring colours. This peculiar nearness I have described in the style of their houses is characteristic of the Basques, and prevails, I am told, throughout their territory.

During fine weather St. Jean de Luz may no doubt assume a more lively and agreeable air than it does just now, owing to the bustle of trade, and quantity of shipping in the harbour. This flourishing town is extremely well supplied by an abundant, though at present expensive market, and hotels, cafés, restaurateurs &c. are almost as numerous as Sterne's barber's shops in Paris, and seem to command an almost equally extensive practice. Every description of sutlers appear to have settled in this place, who, from supplying the necessities of the army, of course derive a pretty thriving trade.

The country surrounding St. Jean de Luz, and its neighbourhood, is beyond measure fine and picturesque. The Pyrenees and lesser hills, with the values formed between them, constitute altogether a most beautiful and interesting country; nor are the attractions of this delightful region confined to inanimate objects alone, for the personal appearance, manners, and character of the people are at least equal to the natural advantages of the territory they inhabit. The whole race, indeed, is of so novel and singular a description, that I should not feel myself justified in passing it over, without giving you a somewhat particular insight into the customs and habits of this peculiar tribe.

Through the whole of the Basque country nothing can exceed the strength and symmetry of the men, and the graceful beauty of the women. These people are perfectly different in their habits and manners, as well as in person and costume, from every other race of men I have hitherto seen. The style of their features is usually aquiline; they, in common, wear their hair long, flowing in curls over their shoulders; and upon their heads the peasantry invariably place a small blue bonnet, precisely resembling that worn by the Scotish highlanders. Their necks and breasts are generally bare, and they wear a blue or brown jacket open, and their breeches loose at the knees, and made to sit easily about the hips. Their legs are usually bare, though they occasionally use gaiters (mostly of leather), furnished with a great number of buttons. They all carry a small stick, curiously worked, upon which they greatly pride themselves; and this they use for defence, as well as to assist them in climbing the tremendous precipices of the country, a task which they perform with a degree of rapidity and agility perfectly surprising. They are capable of sustaining great bodily exertions and privations, and are in the habit of undertaking almost incredible journies on foot. They are much addicted to smoking, and indeed are rarely seen without a pipe. Nothing can exceed the goodness of disposition which the Basques in general possess, and they seem to be quite free from all the predominant vices of the Spanish character. They live a simple life of happiness and content, and being fortunately placed in a country standing in need of little or no cultivation to produce the common necessaries of life, the means of supporting a family are within the reach of every one: a circumstance that promotes early marriages, and in consequence, numerous families of hardy and robust children are produced.

The vallies of the Pyrenees are peculiarly fertile, abounding in picturesque views, which, together with the stupendous precipices, reminded me of Johnson's description of the happy valley in Rasselas.

The Basques affirm their language to be the most ancient in the world, and the original one before the confusion at Babel. That it is in a great degree an original language I have no doubt, but it be of such ancient origin as is pretended, is a question I am not prepared to go into. Certainly among the towns at short distances from that part of the country called the Basque, which must have considerable intercourse with those of the latter, the people are known not to be able to pronounce the Basqueueze language like the Basques themselves.

In addition to their various natural peculiarities, the inhabitants of the Basque country enjoy certain privileges extremely valuable. They are not subject to many of the laws of Spain, especially those relating to taxation. Both Spanish and French Biscay, are in a manner, independent, and not tributary to the monarchs of either country; their territory being a principality or signiory (as it is called), of itself. The tract possessing these advantages and peculiarities extends from Biscay to the neighbourhood of Bordeaux, including a district around Bayonne and the Pyrenees. But, I mm the necessary mixture of people, the dialect in use is consequently as various as the inhabitants; which, by the union of the Gasconne with the Basqueueze, produces a species of patois. While, however, the language becomes mixed, the characteristic distinction of the people remains unaltered. A native Basque is readily known from a Gasconne, from the great superiority of person which the former possesses over the latter.

If you have any curiosity to study the Basque language, I am told the best book upon the subject is a dictionary by Laramendi, a Jesuit, in which the Basqueueze, Castillian, and Latin are compared. It is a rare and difficult book to be procured.

The features of the women are what we should term Grecian, their limbs are finely turned and robust, and they wear their hair turned back from the forehead, and (as I before observed) platted into a long queue, Listened at the bottom by a bow of riband. Their dress is simple and becoming. Those who live in towns usually place an handkerchief over the head and tie it under the chin, and often add a short scarlet cloak, with an hood, similar to the Welch wittle.

In this neighbourhood there is a remarkable mountain at the Pena de Haya, the extreme left of the Pyrenees, which is called the mountain of five crowns. One part of it is split at its summit, into the shape of a bishop's mitre, on which the Basques insist, that the ark remained when the waters subsided, producing this cleft by its pressure.

The Adour

Peyrehorade, March, 1814. As soon as two or three days halting had given time to repair the inconveniencies attendant upon a long march, through bad roads, we continued to advance more into the interior of the country, following the route of the army towards Toulouse. Bayonne being possessed by the enemy, and the high road passing too near to the walls of the town, made it necessary for us to pursue our way through by-roads and lanes, deemed by the natives (especially at this season of the year) absolutely impassable and it excited no small degree of astonishment, when they beheld a brigade wading through mud in many places up to the horses' bellies, with occasional deep holes, that rendered the march both difficult and dangerous; nor was it till we regained the high road that any other species of ground was met with.

Before we entered this town nothing but small detached villages presented themselves, with a few old chateaus deserted by their rightful owners, and divested of every thing resembling their ancient hospitality. Upon our march to the village of Biarotte we crossed the river Adour, so conspicuous in the history of this campaign for the many difficulties overcome in the recent passage of our troops over it, at a season of the year when the rapidity of the stream, swollen by the wintry torrents, was considered as an insurmountable obstacle to our advance, on the part of the enemy. At the time we crossed the river the floods had subsided, and a bridge of boats, since erected, secured an easy passage lo the brigade. After passing this bridge, and a strong and well-built pier, extending a considerable way along the side of the river, forming a communication with the high road, a fine view is obtained of Bayonne about two miles inland. As far as I could judge from this distance, it appeared to be a well fortified town with a strong castle in its centre. Around this neighbourhood there are extensive and barren plains of sand, upon the banks of the Adour. After crossing these, and wading through a succession of muddy lanes, it afforded us no small gratification to find ourselves once again on the high road, which, however, the late rains, and the passing armies, had reduced generally to a very indifferent state. Our arrival at the neat, small, and highly civilized town of Peyrehorade, gave us no small satisfaction and the weather clearing up, afforded more cheering prospects of this delightful country than we had hitherto witnessed. This town lies upon the banks of the Adour, and the surrounding country again becomes fertile and interesting. This is the first completely French town I have been in, and, compared with those of Spain in general, forms a striking contrast; the appearance of the people, streets, and houses, affording ideas of a degree of comfort and civilization rarely to be observed in the latter. Peyrehorade is celebrated for its salmon, which abound, in the river adjacent. A mode of fishing for them has been of late years invented, equally novel and ingenious. At different points of the river a pair of large fans, of hollowed net-work, are made to dip alternately in the stream in performing a rotatory motion. A number of fish are in consequence ensnared, and, when arrived at a certain elevation, are propelled through a short passage, constructed for the purpose, into a cylindrical frame of net-work, and thence into a kind of box, so constructed as to instantly close upon the entrance of the fish, where they remain until removed for sale. I was informed, that a person possessing one of these fisheries makes a certain profit of about two hundred pounds sterling annually, which, in this country, is a very handsome income.

An opportunity occurring to send this letter off, obliges me to shorten it, and conclude.

The South of France Campaign

Pau, April, 1814. Since my last letter we have continued to advance, and every day has furnished fresh objects for admiration. Having been of late so much accustomed to prospects of wild and romantic scenery, with mountains, rocks, ravines, cataracts and water falls, there is something, from contrast, peculiarly pleasing in the contemplation of the opposite species of country by which we are now surrounded. The former scenes, perhaps chiefly from their novelty, certainly excite astonishment, admiration, and interest; but in time, the eye seems to be weary of these, and to feel a relief in beholding the present kind of views, conveying, perceptibly, ideas of comfort and social enjoyments, in which the others fail. The whole of this part of the south of France lies low, yet not so much so as to present a perfect flat appearance, it being every where most beautifully diversified with gently sloping hills, excepting only the grand chain of the Pyrenees, hitherto constantly in view during our route; and which, from its distance, by no means interferes with the rural scenery surrounding us. From the neighbourhood of Bayonne hence the land is greatly employed in the cultivation of vines, which farther westward generally resemble those of the greater part of Portugal, being suffered to grow lull, and run upon high poles, resembling the mode in which hops are trained in our own country. But the mode of cultivating them in these pans begins to approximate to the manner I have seen usually adopted in Spain (particularly in the northern provinces) of cutting them down very low.

Meadows, covered with the finest species of grasses in infinite variety, with uplands adorned with verdure of all descriptions and shades, Intermixed with the most beautiful and richest corn-fields, meet the eye in every direction. The country does not abound in forests, or woods, although it is not deficient in smaller clusters of trees, here and there scattered about. I observed no land absolutely waste, all being cultivated and enclosed to a certain degree, and presenting the idea of a well, though not perhaps, highly tilled district; forming indeed, as I am told, a tolerably fair picture of agriculture throughout the whole of France.

While, however, I am thus led to admire the beauties of the country, which scarcely any circumstances can obliterate, I cannot forbear to mingle with these observations facts that do not present themselves in so fascinating a light. Whatever advantages to the community at large, the revolution may have brought about, there can be no doubt of the individual misery which it has pretty widely distributed; the evils of which, it must indeed require many years of happiness, in the most extended sense of the word, to atone for and counterbalance. The national vanity of the people has been flattered by the achievements of the extraordinary man who now possesses the supreme direction of the empire. But, how dear have they not paid for the gratification of this ruling passion? The population has been so entirely drained by the numerous and heavy conscriptions that have taken place, that none but women, elderly men, and children are to be met with in general; and the miserable inhabitants of every village and town, where their own army has been stationed, have been so long harrassed by requisitions and oppressions of every description, that they are left nearly destitute of every common means of subsistence and comfort. I have mostly witnessed, among the people upon whom I happened to have been quartered, that they felt it to be a real relief, whenever portions of the British army took up their quarters among them, uniformly regarding us more in the light of friends, than of conquering enemies. Their own armies, they have often said, were indeed the foes which they chiefly dreaded; for not content with pillaging, plundering, and oppressing them, they tore the dearest relations from the bosoms of their families, or demanded such sums for their ransom as entailed misery and ruin upon their devoted heads.

Yet notwithstanding the depressed condition of the people in this quarter of France, and their distance from the capital, there is certainly a very striking superiority to be noticed among them, when compared with the nation which I have recently quitted. A better insight into every thing which regards the comforts of life, and a greater degree of hospitality pretty generally pervades every description of people that I have hitherto been acquainted with in the country. To these advantages they unite a degree of liveliness and suavity of manners, coupled with a neatness in their persons and dress, which, upon the first acquaintance, cannot fail to render them interesting and agreeable to every one; and particularly so to those, who, like myself, have recently left a country of so very opposite a description in all these particulars. I have often remarked it as forming one of the leading defects of the Spaniards, that they will not put themselves out of their way to serve any one, in whose views they are not immediately interested; but here, on the contrary, I have noticed, and experienced myself, every description of those little nameless kindnesses that tend to smooth the passage through life, and to bind man and man together by firmer bonds, than perhaps actions of a more exalted nature, which must of necessity be of much less frequent occurrence.

The women, however, have some few customs among them, which, according to our ideas of female delicacy, create no inconsiderable drawback upon their personal attractions. The masculine habit of riding a-stride, which I believe is more or less prevalent throughout France, is very common here, among the generality of people; and, as they have no peculiar dress adapted for the purpose, the ungracefulness of the custom appears still more offensive to the eyes of an Englishman; for when in full gallop, they really reminded me of the female knights errant of Ariosto. Another custom in practice among them is yet more objectionable and offensive. Both the young and old are in the habit of putting issues in their arms or legs, upon the score of health, although they may be absolutely free at the time from any species of complaint whatever. The origin of this strange custom I am at a loss to discover. It may possibly arise from a somewhat similar prejudice to that which induces the lower orders of people in our own country to be bled regularly every spring and fall. But, from whatever cause it proceeds, it is one of the most disagreeable and loathsome habits I have witnessed. Of the superior class of females we have seen none, and very few beyond the rank of shopkeepers. My experience, indeed, has not gone much farther, with regard to men of the first description, though the latter are somewhat more frequently to be seen than the former. Two predominant foibles are conspicuously common to both sexes—excessive vanity, and a never-ceasing disposition to chatter, accompanied by a corresponding aversion from every species of thinking.

In a former part of my letters, I noticed the superiority of the

French Basque peasantry, over the generality of the Spanish peasants. But this is applicable to the Basques only. The male Gasconnes, though certainly endowed with higher degrees of intellectual power, are much inferior to the Spaniards in strength of body, and masculine appearance. The females also fall below those of the latter nation in beauty and symmetry of person, as much as the Basque women excel the Spanish. With regard to the intellectual powers of the French, I have often been much amused in witnessing instances of the ingenuity, and energy of character displayed even by the lowest orders of the French army, when they fell into our hands. The careless air with which they support their misfortunes, and the heroic patience which they display, under trials of all descriptions, is really to be scarcely paralleled in the school of Epictetus.

The next town of importance to Peyrehorade which lay in our way was Orthes; a name now familiar to every English ear, and which must for ever be celebrated in the annals of our country. It is an extensive and handsome town, and very populous. We rested here only a few hours, during which time I employed myself in seeing the place. It was market-day, and the quantity of buyers and sellers that thronged the streets was very great. Poultry of all kinds, game, eggs, fruit, vegetables, and meat were in great abundance; and when compared with the markets we had hitherto seen, was really magnificent; and the articles were excessively cheap, and much below the standard of the best English markets, though somewhat above the rate of those places which the British troops had not visited, in force enough to raise considerably the price of provisions.

From Orthes we next marched into this town, where we are now halting. The approach to it, by the suburbs and adjacent country, prepare the traveller for meeting with a considerable place. After passing over a fine bridge, the road leads into the main street, which is nearly two miles in length, and is adorned on either side with very respectable and handsome houses. The inhabitants appear to be particularly sociable and well inclined towards the English. A neat little theatre, where comedies are performed, stands in the upper part of the town; but, owing to its being Passion Week, it was not attended by many of the inhabitants, the greater part of the audience consisting almost entirely of strangers passing through the town.

In a large nunnery, situated upon the skirts of the town, an extensive hospital is formed for the relief of sick and wounded soldiers. It is attended by the medical men of the place gratuitously, assisted by the kind offices of the only useful order of nuns that I have heard of, Les Sœurs de la Charité. The great degree of neatness, and attention to the comforts of the sick, displayed throughout the whole arrangement of the hospital, is very gratifying, and is seldom equalled in our country although I am inclined to believe that the professional attendants are far less skilful, and not so well informed as those of our hospitals in general. Notwithstanding we are in a state of warfare with the nation, our soldiers are admitted into this excellent charity, and provided for with the greatest degree of humanity. The principal curiosity of the town is the chateau of Henry IV now in a state of ruin. Part of his chambers, and the knives and forks which he used, are still preserved, and shown to visitors.

The neighbourhood of Pau is remarkably fine, and must have been very populous when the inhabitants were suffered to remain undisturbed possessors of their estates.

Several chateaus are to be seen in the neighbourhood, the owners of which have long since fled from the ravages of the revolution, or have forfeited their lives upon the guillotine, because they supported and formed a part of the aristocracy of the country. The appearance of these ancient edifices brings to the recollection the feudal days of England. A chateau, properly so called, was originally the castle or residence of the Lords of the adjacent district, being usually somewhat fortified, and surmounted with turrets; though in modern days the term has been, by courtesy, applied indiscriminately to the habitations of any country gentlemen of fortune and consequence.

The waters of Pau, formerly so celebrated, are not found in the town, but at some distance in the neighbourhood. They are fallen, as I am informed, into neglect and disuse.

Toulouse

Cantonments near Toulouse, April, 1814. After a sufficient halt at Pau, we proceeded to the neighbourhood of Toulouse, where we are now awaiting for orders. Upon our route we met numerous conscripts deserting from the French army, happy in the opportunity afforded them of returning to their homes, under the protection which the advance of the British afforded.

At Ibos, a large and straggling village upon the road, next to Pau, I was lodged in the house of a wealthy farmer, a respectable American, who showed me many civil attentions, being acquainted with some of my friends in the West Indies. In common with many others of his countrymen, he had purchased considerable lands, and settled in France, his estate being chiefly dedicated to the cultivation of grapes. He complained very much of the deficiency of labourers, in consequence of the conscription, and other effects of the war, which had materially impoverished his farms.

The next considerable town in our way was Tarbes, which, though large and populous, is inferior in every other respect to Pau. Great quantities of wine and brandy are made in this district, which is considered one of (he most flourishing parts of the south of France. Nearly opposite to this place, the highest mountains of the Pyrenees are seen, the chain declining in elevation to the right and left. Near the town of Tarbes, upon an elevation commanding an almost boundless prospect stands a monument, erected in honor of the Emperor and Empress Josephine, upon the occasion of their passing this way, about six years ago, to Spain and Portugal. Proceeding through the small towns of Rebastens and Mirande, we arrived at the city of Auch, a very large, populous, and handsome place. The collegiate church is a magnificent and spacious edifice, adorned beautifully on the outside with line specimens of gothic ornaments highly deserving of notice. The interior is no less splendidly fitted up, having an excellent organ, accompanied by a very superior choir of singers. The commune, for the transaction of the public business of the town, is a very elegant building.

After halting some time, at the neat little town of Gimont, and at L'Isle en Jourdain, in the neighbourhood of Toulouse, we arrived at our present cantonments, that have nothing to recommend them but a very fine chateau in which I am quartered, belonging to one of Buonaparte's generals, and furnished in the most elegant style.

At L'Isle en Jourdain, we received the gratifying intelligence of Soult's flight from Toulouse, and the entrance of our army into the town. The sensation produced among the inhabitants at this news was very striking. They exhibited evident signs of satisfaction at what they considered to be the death-blow to his army.—At any rate, the change must have been beneficial to the neighbouring towns and villages, as all communication with Toulouse had been cut off for some time past, and a stop put to the great commercial intercourse subsisting before the arrival of the contending armies.

Soon after we arrived here, intelligence was received of the change of affairs that had taken place in Paris, with which you must have long ago been apprised; as it appears, that the dispatches, intended to announce to us the new state of things, have been intercepted, and for a time delayed.

What a criminal desire for mischief must have existed among the agents of Buonaparte, to have induced them to obstruct the circulation of news, which had for its object the suspension of hostilities, the continuation of which, under existing circumstances, could not be productive of the slightest advantage? The effect of this interception though it has added again to the renown of the British arms, must ever be lamented as the cause of a needless loss of gallant and brave men on both sides.

Immediately upon the arrival of the Paris bulletin, 1 took an opportunity of visiting Toulouse. It is a very large and populous town, and if the accounts of the inhabitants may be relied on, it is certainly the fourth city in France. The entrance on the western side, across a large and handsome bridge, thrown over the Garonne, is very striking, but I was much disappointed with the rest of the town. The streets are all very narrow, and, as usual, few of them are furnished with paved footways; the houses too, in general, being small, and shabby in their appearance.—They have shops, however, in abundance, through the town, which, generally speaking, are very excellent, especially those of the booksellers and jewellers.

After crossing the bridge, to the right and left, a long range of public buildings, consisting of warehouses &c. on the banks of the river, produces somewhat of the appearance of grandeur; but this I think forms the only fine view in Toulouse; every other part bears a dirty, confined, and rather mean look for a town of such note and importance.

There is but one square in the place, that exhibits any thing like grandeur, and this is dedicated to the public market. One side of it is filled up by the Capitolium, a name which is derived from the title of the chief magistrate of the town, who is termed "Le Capitoul." It is a very elegant and spacious edifice of white stone, built in the modern style of architecture. Some handsome pillars front the building, which is ornamented with carved work, the word, 'Capitolium' being written in large golden letters over the centre balcony. The apartments are dedicated to the business of the city, and public entertainments: one of them is constructed for an hall of audience, and a splendid throne of crimson velvet, and gold embroidery, with the crown of Buonaparte on the summit of the canopy, is placed at the head of it, with two chairs for the Emperor and Empress; and it was here that they received the addresses of the people, as they passed through Toulouse on their way to Spain.

This place is what Buonaparte (for the great devotion it has always manifested in his cause) used to number among his 'good cities.' At the lower end of one of the principal rooms a bust of Napoleon lately stood, which, on the change of affairs, was hurled by the populace out of the windows into the streets, with cries of *"à bas le tyran; vive les Bourbons,"* &c.

Every person in Toulouse wears the white cockade. The English mount it upon the black one worn by the military, while the French officers mount the black cockade upon the white, in compliment to us. I trust that this sudden and universal assumption of the lily, springs from the heart, and does not arise from mere fashion and whim. I am inclined to believe, that the people about these parts are really sincere in their expressions of satisfaction at the restoration of the Bourbons, whatever may be the present state of the national feeling farther north.

The usual demonstrations of joy have been taking place, viz, illuminations, public entertainments &c. and our illustrious hero receives honors, which, in pagan days, would have at least elevated him to the rank of a demigod. The present population of Toulouse is estimated at about fifty thousand, the chief portion of which is engaged in trade.

After Hostilities Cease

Cantonments, near Toulouse, April, 1814. I shall now renew the subjects which I was unable to finish in my last letter relative to Toulouse. The female part of the community in this town, lies under a somewhat similar stigma to that which used to be visited upon their fair sisters in our renowned city of Bristol, who (it is, said) were in former days celebrated for a proverbial deficiency of beauty and grace. I am not aware of the French legislature having deemed it necessary to interfere upon so serious an occasion, whatever might have been judged expedient by the English parliament, with respect to the Litter devoted place; where it appears to have been thought politically adviseable, to offer certain extra rewards and incitements to marriage, lest the absence of other attractions should have condemned the town to perpetual celibacy. It certainly might seem hard to visit an whole race with this sweeping clause; but, I must say, from my own experience, I could not help charitably hoping, that, as Providence is generally impartial in his dispensations, he may have made up at Toulouse, in the score of amiability, for the lamentable deficiency of personal charms. And judging by this rule, the shrine of virtue, at this place, must have no ordinary number of Votaries. Their hideous mode of dressing themselves, also, by no means lends to assist in improving the parsimony of nature, towards this much Injured class. High-heeled and pointed shoes, long waists, and enormous bonnets, nearly one third of the height of the body, with several piles of ribbons, row above row, upon the crown, and long streaming sashes about the middle, altogether create an appearance, which, in its toute ensemble, I should think absolutely without a parallel. You must not suppose, from this description, that I am so decided a John Bull, as to fancy there are no ladies deserving of praise out of our own country; although for the most part, I have reason to believe, from what I have seen, that I am justified in giving an undoubted preference to my own country women. In spite, however, of all this, as is generally the case, some improvement might be gathered from a comparison even with decided inferiority. From what I have hitherto seen of the French ladies, they possess a quickness and vivacity of manner which render them amusing, notwithstanding the many defects of their character. This, and their minute attention to what is termed *les petits soins de la vie*, gives them attractions from which our ladies might learn an useful lesson.

It may be objected, that this disposition, which indeed predominates among both sexes, borders on insincerity, and a lightness of character, totally incompatible, with real feeling and integrity. I certainly should not for a moment venture to compare the ladies of the two nations together, but it does appear to me that an union of the manners of both might be somewhat preferable to either of them, separately taken. To finish this general, though imperfect sketch of Toulouse, it only remains for me to remark, that there are abundance of hotels, cafes &c. many of which are very elegantly fitted up, and in a style greatly superior to those which are to be met with, generally, in London, and perhaps better adapted to the taste and manners of the French; for, an Englishman of business, wrapped up in mercantile speculations, who frequently enters a coffee-house for the double motive of gratifying his hunger and arranging his thoughts, would find himself lamentably off in the cafe of a French restaurateur; and he would no doubt prefer a plain beef-steak at Dolly's, or even at John-a-Groat's, where he might enjoy his potatoes hot, and his thoughts undisturbed. The gay and lively inhabitants of France resort in crowds to these places of refreshment, apparently devoid of care, and more, as it would appear, from the desire of amusement, than the satisfying of their hunger. Of all the confusion of tongues I have ever experienced, a French coffee-house exhibits the most extraordinary display, and certainly since the destruction of the Tower of Babel nothing can have ever been like it in the world. To this eternal jabbering, which is pretty general in these places throughout France, may be added, at Toulouse, a never-ceasing succession of beggars, pedlars, tumblers, conjurors &c. who are admitted into the cafes, from an importunity requiring no small share of resolution to resist. These gentry carry their impudence to the most extraordinary pitch, infesting your table while at dinner, and forcing their various sorts of merchandize upon you, consisting chiefly of toys, trinkets, laces &c. and often of articles more exceptionable though not less marketable. A similar species of persecution is practiced by the jugglers, who are equally numerous and importunate. Happening to dine at one of these places, upon my first arrival, I was not a little astonished by a female, attended by two little girls, entering the room; and, without ceremony, directly proceeding to unburthen themselves of a considerable portion of their upper vestments, so as to give me some apprehensions for the conclusion of the business, the meaning of which I was totally at a loss to conjecture. I was however soon relieved from my alarm, by perceiving the woman, accompanied by the two children, proceed to tumble over several times up and down the whole length of the room, between the tables, walk upon their hands, and perform various other feats of agility, and concluding the whole, as usual, by a demand upon your purse.

Gambling-houses, balls, and the theatre make up the principal public amusements of the evening. The latter is well built, neatly fitted up, and tolerably supported.

The town contains a cathedral and four churches, all of which are handsome buildings. The former is very ancient and spacious, and presents a more venerable aspect than the generality of those which I have hitherto noticed. The remainder are much in the usual French style. They are furnished and ornamented in a less heavy and tawdry manner than those of Portugal and Spain, though with less appearance of grandeur, richness, and wealth.

The country immediately in the vicinity of Toulouse possesses as little beauty as the town itself, being neither interesting in its general appearance nor remarkable for fertility and cultivation, while all the villages around are in a state of poverty and partial devastation. The Garonne sweeps round a portion of the town, and in some spots affords pleasing views, but the chief beauties for which its banks are celebrated lie remote from the city. It is a broad clear, deep, and rapid stream, and is navigable to a considerable distance. A wall encircles the remainder of the town, which is not defended by the river.

These advantages Soult had availed himself of, and kept the inhabitants in great terror by preparations for resistance, which, however, were certainly not of a nature to prevent its destruction, had our army found it necessary to carry it by assault.

I had hoped that the arrival of the late intelligence from Paris would have produced a permanent cessation of hostilities, especially considering the repeated defeats which Soult has latterly sustained and the discontent which is said to prevail throughout his army. But this indefatigable and persevering general, whose exertions would have done honor to a better cause, does not appear at all inclined to avail himself of the fair opportunity he now has of relinquishing this fruitless contest. It is said that he affects to doubt the authenticity of the news relating to his master's overthrow, and expresses a determination to hold out as long as he has any troops to stand by him. In consequence of this declaration his retreat in the direction of the pass of Perpignan is closely followed up, in order to bring him to terms, to which no doubt he will ere long accede.

Putting aside all considerations of the master he serves, and the cause to which he is devoted, there is something noble, and certainly to be admired, in the principle of perseverance and determined resolution, which has been so uniformly displayed throughout the whole conduct of this distinguished general. I am told that Lord Wellington thinks very highly of him as a commander, and I believe the praises of his countrymen do not overrate his merits.

Some of the leading circumstances of Soult's life, which I have obtained from authentic information, may not perhaps be uninteresting to you.

It appears that he is now in about his forty-sixth year, and is one of the four generals of the Imperial Guard. It is said that his military pride is not less than his extreme professional ardor, and that he seems to be perfectly conscious of his great talents. He was born of mean parents, and is indebted to his own exertions for his advancement. At the age of sixteen he enlisted as a private in the army, and in 1792 was raised to the rank of Adjutant-Major of the National Guards. The following year he was appointed Adjutant-General to the army of the Moselle, under Jourdan, and afterwards chief of the staff of Lefebre's division of that army which marched upon the Sambre. In 1794 he particularly distinguished himself at the battle of Fleures, and was himself on that occasion the sole cause of victory to the French. This was followed by his being made General of Brigade, and ultimately he procured Lefebre's division, which he commanded at the battle of Leibtingen, 26th of March, 1799. He was afterwards employed in Switzerland, under Massena, whom he followed into Italy, and assisted at the siege of Genoa, where he was wounded. He next had an army of observation at Naples, and was both beloved and feared by his troops and the inhabitants. His next appointment was to the Colonelcy-General of the Foot Chasseurs of the Consular Guard; for his conduct in which situation, Buonaparte appointed him to the chief command of the Boulogne encampment; and, when this was broken up, he crossed the Rhine at Sprie, in September, 1805, and entered Germany crowned with success; receiving the most flattering approbations from Napoleon for his consummate skill and perseverance, when almost every other general and even his master, was inclined to despair.

After the peace of Tilsit, Soult commanded the army of Spain. In November, 1808, he attacked and destroyed the army of Estramadura, and penetrated into the Asturias, and afterwards fought the battle of Corunna with Sir John Moore. He next, by his march upon Placentia with Mortier, obliged Lord Wellington to relinquish his position at Talavera; and King Joseph employed him as chief of his staff, in the room of Jourdan. On the 19th of November, 1809, Joseph and Soult beat Arrizaja, with 50,000 Spaniards, at Ocana, while the French army did not amount to 30,000, although declared by Buonaparte, some time previously, to be 70,000 strong. On the 20th of January, 1810, Soult's celebrated passage of the Sierra Morena took place, which brings the chief circumstances of that great general's life up to a period, so recent and so well known as to need no farther remarks. It is gratifying to the feelings of Englishmen, and must be a source of proud exultation to our renowned and invincible general, that the former perpetual round of success, which encircled Soult, has been checked in its progress, when he had to contend with British arms.

While I was at Toulouse I saw numbers of the Gardes Nationales, who, no doubt, were far from being displeased, from the nature of their services, in the opportunity lately afforded them of mounting the white cockade, and relinquishing their military habits; for which they do not appear, either by natural or acquired taste, to be at all adapted. All are obliged to clothe and equip themselves. They are, however, upon the whole, a fine looking body of men, and seem to be formed of a respectable class of citizens.

At Rest Again

Cantonments, May, 1814. Since I last addressed you from the neighbourhood of Toulouse, we have retraced our steps, and are arrived in these, I presume, our last cantonments in France; where we shall probably remain till arrangements are concluded for our departure for England. Our advance lay at first by the route which Soult had taken, whom our army was pursuing with the utmost rapidity. Upon our march the brigade was reviewed by Lord Wellington, in a field near Toulouse; and a number of the townspeople, assembled on this occasion, saluted the Duke with the usual mode of approbation. A few days past they were, no doubt, equally vociferous in favour of Soult and Napoleon. While advancing, at a short distance from Toulouse, we met the second in command of the French army, very superbly dressed, in a coach and four, and escorted by a party of hussars, upon his way to our head-quarters, in order to make arrangements for a cessation of hostilities; and, on the day following, we received the order to halt. A very splendid ball and supper was given in the Capitolium on this occasion, at which the Duke of Wellington presided, seated in the chair, and beneath the canopy which had been originally prepared for Buonaparte. The sight of the illustrious hero upon this truly gratifying event, when the enthusiasm of the people was at the highest pitch, produced the most animating feelings; and the company may literally be said to have been intoxicated with joy, when his Lordship descended from the throne, and walked down the room, the people shouting, clapping their hands, and flinging their hats in the air; while the females waved their white handkerchiefs, and the room re-echoed with cries of *"vive Lord Wellington"* &c.

Nothing can exceed the hospitality and kind attention with which we have been received every where on our march hither. Our way lay frequently through towns and villages, unaccustomed to the dreadful visitation of the soldiery, in that degree to which many others have been exposed; and this may in some measure account for the kindness we experienced. The people expressed no small astonishment in beholding the train of animals, and the quantity of baggage attendant upon our march.—They had been accustomed to see their own army live at almost free-quarters, in every place they marched through, upon the peaceful and unoffending inhabitants, as a matter of course; rendering thereby the attendance of servants, and the inconvenience of baggage unnecessary, which, under our liberal and more politic system of campaigning, became indispensably requisite. While, however, this mode of proceeding procured to the British army the esteem and respect of the inhabitants in general, it became an endless source of jealousy to our opponents' force; which not only found itself subdued in the field, but also completely outdone in generosity. Wherever we went the people welcomed us, and hailed us as their deliverers and friends; while the French troops, even in their native country, experienced a species of humiliation and degradation in the opinions of their own fellow-citizens.

Their leader dethroned, and their more immediate prospects annihilated, I fear they mount the white cockade from feelings of necessity, rather than from a conviction of the justice of the cause; and this is a sentiment too natural to be easily and quickly removed. An immense mass of the population is interested in warfare, which neither the want of success, nor the destruction of their armies can speedily remove. Thousands have thriven from it, and they are, of course, attached to the cause of the person who supported it; putting aside that natural restlessness inherent in the French character, which at no time can easily accommodate itself to the "piping times of peace," especially, when that peace has been forced upon them, which has originated in humbled pride and absolute defeat.

Let not our friends at home congratulate themselves too fondly upon this general cry in favour of the Bourbons and of peace. However agreeable it may be to the English, and conducive to the repose of the world, to witness the late scourge of Europe fallen to the dust; yet, a very slight acquaintance only with the French and their history, will sufficiently point out the absurdity of supposing that these ideas can meet the heart of every Frenchman, or by any means unite the feelings of the country in one general bond of amity favourable to the allies.

In the midst of that chaos, which has been the result of the breaking up of all parties, we can look for consolation alone, from the single circumstance arising out of the physical inability of the kingdom to make any farther resistance.

I should very much doubt, whether, at this moment, France may not be laughing in her sleeves at the affected moderation of the Emperor Alexander, in sparing the city of Paris, and the lives of the extraordinary being and his associates, who have recently conducted the energies of this powerful nation; and, from whose activity, ability, and disappointed ambition, the most formidable and decided hostility may be apprehended. Nor will partizans be wanting, whenever opportunity offers of again rallying round the standard of one, whose exploits so greatly contributed to the gratification of the vanity, and nationality of the French character.

Upon our road to this place, we met the Duc d'Angouleme, accompanied by the Count de Gramont, upon their journey to Paris. Our brigade opened right and left to permit the procession to pass, and to pay the usual ceremonies due to a prince. Nothing could exceed the display of enthusiasm and affection which he experienced from the different towns and villages through which he passed. The people appeared really intoxicated with joy, and every individual seemed to vie with the other in making all necessary preparations for the occasion. All the houses were decorated with white flags, intermixed with evergreens; and triumphal arches formed of festoons, and emblems of the lily were thrown over the entrances of the different villages through which he rode; the principal people uniformly going out on horseback full-dressed, adorned with the Croix de St. Louis, and white scarfs, to welcome his approach. In the evening, illuminations, balls &c. followed.

You have, no doubt, experienced, in the middle of all these prosperous events, a considerable damp, from the unfortunate business that has occurred at Bayonne; which, when considered as the final close of an unexampled career of victory and glory, is, from the circumstances under which it happened, peculiarly to be lamented.

France

Cantonments, May, 1814. I am very much pleased with the country about this place, which affords the most agreeable rides and walks, and delightful scenery. It is more diversified with hill and dale than any that I have hitherto seen, and the scenery is every where enriched with fine woods, and whatever can constitute a pleasing prospect. The windings of the Garonne every where form the leading features of the country, which is also enriched with a larger proportion of meadow land, than is generally found in these parts.

It is, however, very obvious, that this apparently rich and fertile country is capable of being considerably improved. A British farmer, unacquainted with the dreadful effects of an actual state of war, would feel much contempt at the appearance of the land and crops, when put in competition with those of his own country, flourishing under all the advantages of agricultural skill, and a free government, accompanied by internal tranquillity.

I understand that it is the intention of landholders, to turn their views, in future, more to the growth of corn than to the culture of vines; which is at present their principal object. If they can procure a sufficient market for the former, there will be a plentiful source of employment for the immense increase in population, which the return of the prisoners from Russia and England, must unavoidably create. A considerable quantity of corn is every where grown, but it is for the most part poor and spare, from the very indifferent manner in which the land is tilled and manured. An inadequate demand, and the great scarcity of labourers, have hitherto been esteemed the causes of this general deficiency in cultivation.

The internal resources of France are immense, and I think I may hazard the conjecture, that they are fully adequate to her consumption, if properly managed. While she has been grasping at extension of territory, she has neglected her own internal advantages. Her population has been so drained, to secure foreign possessions, that she has impoverished those lands which alone are her rightful inheritance. Having resigned her ambitious projects upon the former, without securing the prosperity of the latter, she now finds herself in a state of poverty and misery, which must require many years to remove completely, and to restore her to that exhalted situation which she formerly held among the nations of the world. The French are a people by no means calculated to rest quietly for any length of time together, more especially when peace has brought with it neither victory nor advantage.

I shall now quit these speculations, and return to the delightful country by which we are encircled. Upon the left bank of the river Garonne, near our present quarters, the city of Agen forms a very desirable place of residence, but which the terms of our treaty with Soult forbid British troops to occupy. The streets are neat though not wide, and there is the usual deficiency of pavement for the accommodation of foot-passengers. The shops, and houses in general are above mediocrity, and many of the latter are of a very superior size and construction, forming the abodes chiefly of persons of rank and property. Agen possesses a very handsome cathedral church, and a fine old episcopal palace. The prefect of the department resides in this town, in a very magnificent building.

The theatre is small but very neatly fitted up; and near the town stands a very elegant building, which is dedicated to the reception of the sick and wounded of the army, as well as the lower classes of the community. Its establishment, as well as its structure, is remarkable for its magnificence. The approach to this town, which lies through a beautiful country admirably cultivated, and abound in wood, verdure &c. is by means of an horse-ferry; and the river Garonne, being very rapid, is not crossed without some difficulty and considerable inconvenience. It is indeed a singular circumstance that there should every where, as far as I have observed, be so great a deficiency of bridges in France; whereas in Spain, so much behind France in other points, bridges are thrown over the rivers wherever they are required, while ferry-boats form the frequent substitute for the former in this country. Before you enter the town, on the southwestern side, you have to pass along a very wide, straight, and excellent road, flanked on each side by a row of fine elms, which is so thickly planted as to form a delightful shade the whole way. This avenue extends nearly two miles, and is supposed to be one of the finest in the country. There are also, on each side, smaller roads, for the accommodation of horsemen and foot-passengers. This noble avenue leads into the public walks, forming the most delightful promenade near the banks of the Garonne; altogether constituting the pride and boast of the town, and to which the inhabitants say there is nothing superior of the kind in France.

The Duc d'Angouleme, on his way to Bourdeaux, lately passed through this city, where the usual preparations of triumphal arches, and emblems of the lily, illuminations &c. were prepared for his reception, accompanied by the most enthusiastic demonstrations of joy. A ball was given in the theatre on this occasion, which was attended by all the principal people of the town and neighbourhood amongst whom were several of the old noblesse, and others, who seemed overcome with joy in being able once again to wear the decoration of the lily and the croix de St. Louis, after a lapse of more than twenty years, during which period they had not dared to exhibit these honors.

In this neighbourhood the various sports of fishing, shooting, hunting &c. may be enjoyed in the most complete manner, by those who take delight in these diversions. I shall conclude this letter with a few observations upon the manners of the French, so far as I have hitherto had an opportunity of observing them, and endeavour to give you a slight sketch of the state of society.—You probably have remarked that, upon quitting Spain, I spoke in raptures of the decided superiority of the French over the Spaniards; the former possessing more ease and vivacity, and exhibiting uniformly more hospitable and friendly attentions to strangers than the latter. I also noticed, that the French, while they possessed greater intellectual powers were more civilized and attentive to the domestic concerns of life, and certainly more industrious and active. Though I am convinced, that, from all we have heard of France in former days the events of the last twenty years have diminished much of the respectability of their ancient character, and left little else remaining beyond the shadow of better limes. Urbanity, and what is called the *savoir vivre*, appear to be nearly banished from French society; for it is impossible to look upon their good humour, vivacity, and civil attentions in either of these lights. The men are negligent and dirty in their dress and persons, and possess a coarseness and vulgarity in their manners bordering often upon rudeness. The refinement of the *vieil cour* seems altogether to have passed away, without having been succeeded by any thing more desirable. Boots, a coloured neck-cloth, hair without powder, and the hat seldom removed from the head, even in company, are indiscriminately worn in morning walks and evening parties. All the little niceties and distinctions in dress seem to be disregarded, and the coarse and absurd revolutionary system of equality seems to sanction and excuse a boorishness and indifference to manner, approaching frequently to downright rudeness, and a total inattention to the feelings of others.

With respect to the other sex, whose habits and customs, from necessity, depend very much on those of the former, I have only to observe, that they derogate in a still greater degree from those refinements, both in dress and behaviour, which we are accustomed to consider as forming the great charm of the female character. Neither is there that selection, and distinction of rank kept up among them in their evening assemblies, which common etiquette requires, and which alone can insure propriety and decorum of manners.

From every thing that I can observe, the former excellencies of the French nation, with regard to the subject I have last dwelt upon, have fallen into decay and they are indeed no longer the same people, offering now but few pretensions to that fascinating character which once rendered them so highly celebrated. The absence too of all heart and feeling, which, in former times, characterized the women of France, is now, from the extinction of their former blandishments, rendered still more unamiable and odious. When I say this, you must understand that I am speaking generally. There are, undoubtedly, numerous exceptions to be found, and I myself have, in the course of my journey, discovered many.

A Journey North

Orleans, June, 1814. Since my last letter we have bid farewell to our cantonments, and friends among whom we had resided some weeks; who did not appear to relish the probability of our being succeeded by French troops, whose character does not seem to be held in very high estimation, even in the opinions of their own fellow-citizens.

The necessary arrangements having been completed, for removing the British cavalry from this part of the country to Boulogne and Calais, and thence to England, they were in consequence divided into two columns; in order to avoid the inconvenience attendant upon so large a body as the whole passing by the same route. Our brigade forms a division of that column which takes the road from Toulouse to Paris, to a certain distance; when, leaving that city to the right, we are to pass to Boulogne, by a route hereafter to be issued, which it is supposed we may complete about the middle of July. The motives for this unexpected measure, are, as usual, unknown to us, but various conjectures upon the matter are of course afloat; among which, the avoiding a long sea voyage appears to be one of the most probable, as the injury sustained by horses in a protracted voyage, with all its numerous inconveniencies, is not to be put in competition with a long march, where troops can advance upon a regular system, without distressing either the horses or the men. Perhaps too, in an economical point of view, this plan may have its advantages. The route is sent, I understand, from the office of the French Secretary at War, and orders have been accordingly transmitted to the French troops, occupying places through which we have to pass, to evacuate I heir stations, and afford every facility to our progress.

The first part of our advance was long, tedious, and fatiguing, and peculiarly so as it was performed during very hot weather. It has, however, latterly been attended with much less fatigue and inconvenience, owing, in a great measure, to the weather having become much cooler. We find that as we proceed the leagues vary, and become shorter. In the former parts of the country through which we traversed they were very long, and still less defined.

By referring to the map, you will perceive that we have followed a very irregular and circuitous course, and by no means pursued the direct way; for, after three or four days hard marching, we arrived at a few miles distance only from the place from which we set out. This probably arose in some respects from convenience, but more particularly (a circumstance that I have already pointed out in travelling through this country,) from the great scarcity of bridges which prevails in almost every department we have traversed.

We have passed through several respectable towns upon our road, though at the same time we have occasionally been put to great shifts, by being forced to take up our quarters in small and ill-supplied villages.

From the town of Beaumont (a very neat and considerable town, eight leagues from the place of our starting,) we passed through Grenade and Toulouse to Fennouillet. At the first of these we experienced very hospitable attentions, but in the second we met with very different treatment; which, unfortunately, proved a sample only of that which we have subsequently experienced. This place has been exhausted by the numerous soldiery recently quartered upon it. Most of the better houses (of which there are many,) are vacated; and in the few that are still inhabited, the people appear to care little about us, their chief anxiety being to get rid of us as quickly as possible. Fennouillet turned out to be a miserable village, destitute of almost every comfort of life.

We next passed through Grisolles and Montauban. The former is a tolerable country town, which we arrived at on the 4th of June, and celebrated the King's birthday, with that degree of festivity and loyalty usual on such occasions. The latter city is one of the finest I have seen, and certainly forms a very desirable residence. It stands on an elevated position upon the river Tarn, which winds beneath it, through verdant meadows and woods, in a most beautiful manner. The whole country around is extremely fertile, and exhibits rich and extensive scenery. The city itself is somewhat less in size than Toulouse, but far superior in the neatness and beauty of the streets and houses, wearing altogether an appearance of respectability and fashion which does not belong to the latter. The collegiate church is a noble and spacious building. The theatre, hotels, cafes, restaurateurs &c. are also upon a superior scale. An handsome bridge is thrown across the Tarn, by which the city is entered; and the river, making a sweep through the place, divides it into two parts, distinguished by the names of the new and the old town. The Tarn is less clear and wide than the Garonne, but its banks are peculiarly picturesque. We have found that the general aspect of the country has improved as we have advanced from Toulouse; and it approaches nearer to the beauty of that which I have already described in the neighbourhood of the Pyrenees. The roads, in like manner, become better as we proceed farther into the country.

The route to Caussade (which place has nothing in itself particularly to recommend it,) is sheltered by rows of lofty poplars. In this small town the majority of the inhabitants are Protestants; and a plain church is established there, built by some of our countrymen, and in which the service is performed according to the Protestant rites.

To Cahors our road was again flanked by rows of fine poplars. This part of the country is celebrated for wine, and is of course surrounded on all sides by numerous vineyards, growing in an apparently barren soil, for the most part stony, and lying chiefly on the sides and tops of hills; a species of land which I am told is very favourable to the growth of vines. The wine is the best I have met with in France, and very similar to that made about Bourdeaux. The generality of the country wine elsewhere is scarcely drinkable, being thin, light, and very acidulous. The wine which is generally in use in Portugal and Spain is far superior to that which is commonly drank in France. The country around Cahors is not at all interesting, being less productive in wood, grasses &c. than that which we have recently left.

The next stage to Cahors the country improves again, and becomes daily more delightful and varied as you approach the town of Brives, previously to which we did not meet with any place of note. Brives is situated in a beautiful valley surrounded by one of the finest countries I have seen, consisting of verdant and woody hills, richly diversified with corn, vines, the variously coloured grasses (peculiar to France), and every other requisite tending to form an enchanting landscape. The view of the town, previously to descending from the hills, presents one of the most favourable prospects of it which can be afforded.—Many of the houses are built completely in the country style, and detached from each other; they are also generally roofed with blue slate, and are neatly white-washed. It was no inconsiderable disappointment to me, to find this flattering prospect, of one of the prettiest looking towns I have ever seen, when viewed from a distance, possessing nothing to recommend it within its walls; the streets being narrow, dirty, and confined, and most of the houses small and mean. This inconvenience is somewhat compensated, however, by a very fine promenade, flanked with large lives on each side, encircling the town, while another favourite walk through a rich meadow, by the side of a clear river, contributes much to the beauty and comfort of the place. Hence, to Limoges, the general aspect of the country continues picturesque, interesting, and very abundant in wood; the chessnut, the cherry-tree, and the oak, being the most common.

The city of Limoges is very considerable, spacious and populous. A number of manufactories for cottons, silks, hosiery &c. of all kinds, are here established; which are in a more flourishing condition than those of any town I have visited in France. The streets are mostly wide, clean, and handsome; and it contains several open spaces, and tolerable squares.

The houses are generally very lofty, and many of them are built in a very superior style. The public buildings are all extensive, and possess some degree of grandeur. Among the latter, the Hôtel de Prefecture, and the bishop's palace, form the most distinguished, the last of which exhibits a noble appearance. Its apartments are spacious, and elegantly furnished in the antique style, and adorned with several fine paintings, and other appropriate ornaments; which, together with extensive gardens, and beautiful lawns, laid out in a very tasteful manner, render it a most delightful place.

All the churches have an handsome appearance without, but their interior decorations, with the exception of the cathedral, are less complete. The hotels, cafes, and restaurateurs, are all very elegantly fitted up, and have mostly attached to them gardens for promenades and refreshment.

The chief object of curiosity, in this manufacturing town, and upon which the inhabitants principally pride themselves, is that for porcelain, where I observed many very beautiful and elegant specimens; the ornaments of which were admirably finished, though the substance of the ware itself appeared to be of an inferior quality, in general, to that of our best manufactories.

Hence to Chatteauroux, the next considerable town, the country still possesses its woody and picturesque scenery, with a considerable share of cultivation. Upon our road, we met with a squadron of the Imperial Guard of Maria Louisa, on its march to the southern provinces. It is a very fine regiment, and was the last which quitted the Empress's person. The mens' appointments are suitable to their establishment, but they are not so well mounted, as might have been naturally expected in so distinguished a corps. They are all above the common stature, and wear brass helmets, ornamented with horse-hair; their uniform is green, with buff-facings, jack-boots &c.

As we advance towards the north, our marches become shorter, and the leagues yet more definite and small.

The town of Chatteauroux is large and straggling, and appears to be the most stupid and uninteresting place I have seen throughout the course of our journey.

To Orleans, our route lay generally through a flat country, though not less agreeable than that which we had recently traversed. The immediate vicinity of this place is remarkably fine, and the country becomes again varied with hills, and beautiful and extensive woods. An opportunity occurring to dispatch this letter, I shall defer my description of this celebrated city, when I shall, by the leisure afforded from our halt tomorrow, have more time to examine the various circumstances belonging to it worthy of remark.

Towards Paris

Cantonments, close to Paris, July, 1814. The extent of our original route is now completed, and we are, I understand, after a short halt, to shape our course by a fresh route (issued at Orleans) to Boulogne or Calais. It being my intention to spend a short time at Paris, before we embark, I shall occupy the interval, previously to my setting off for the capital, in concluding my account of our march to this place.

The neighbourhood of Orleans is very populous, and indeed abounds with more than common beauties. The approach to the town is unrivalled by any thing I have yet seen, and would grace the finest capital. After crossing the Loire, which, though certainly inferior to the Garonne, is nevertheless surrounded by very picturesque scenery, we entered upon what is called the north of France, this river forming the boundary between the two great divisions of the country. A very extensive, wide, and straight avenue leads, between rows of fine trees, to the entrance of the city, over a large and handsome bridge thrown across the Loire; which is succeeded by the main street, leading up to the centre of the town, a spacious open place, and surrounded by well-built houses. The street is broad and regular, very long, and furnished with an excellent pavement for foot-passengers. The houses are all uniform and lofty, and reminded me very much of the finest parts of Bath. A great many shops, on an enlarged and showy scale, occupy the ground floors of most of the houses. At the north-east corner of the great central square is placed a bronzed statue of Joan of Arc, upon a marble pedestal, embellished with bass reliefs, illustrative of various circumstances connected with the life of that celebrated heroine.

The remainder of the town is distributed into an infinity of streets, the whole forming the appearance of a large, populous, and flourishing city. The major part of the place is quite modern, the fury of the revolution having spread itself through the streets, and destroyed most of the houses.

The present population is estimated at about forty-five thousand, which I believe, is much less than the number that it formerly possessed.

The society of Orleans appears to be one of its greatest advantages. Many persons of gentility reside in the town and neighbourhood, and seem to be very sociably inclined. The English are held in very general estimation among them. There are two considerable manufactories in Orleans worthy of notice. The one for porcelain exhibits a fine assemblage of various specimens. That for the making of silk is the most interesting; consisting in the conversion of offal into good silk, which is then transmitted to Lyons to be made up into the various forms in which it is sold. This factory is worked by a steam engine, of a power equal to that of ninety horses.

About a league and an half from the town, to the north-east, stands an old mansion, built by the famous Lord Bolingbroke, which now exhibit's a very imperfect specimen only, of the exquisite taste of that elegant-minded and accomplished nobleman. The source of the Loire takes its rise in this neighbourhood, and forms an object of general interest. One of the principal buildings worthy of notice, in the town, is the cathedral, the most spacious and elegant edifice of the kind which I have seen in France. I entered it one morning, during the performance of high mass. The body of the church was excessively thronged, and the aisle was occupied by the different ministers of the church, and a company of soldiers under arms, who assisted at the ceremony. This mixture of religious and military pomp was novel; yet, however contrary to our feelings and opinions it may appear, nevertheless, added much to the awe and solemnity of the scene. At the elevation of the host, the commanding officer gave the word, and the men presented arms, dropt upon one knee, and rested the butt-end of their musquets upon the floor, supported by the left hand, while their right touched the peakes of their caps. A flourish of drums and trumpets accompanied the full organ, and a chorus from the band of singers, echoing through the lofty and vaulted roof of the cathedral, produced a very grand and sublime effect.

On our journey from Orleans to our present head-quarters, we passed through no town of note but the country is exceedingly fine throughout, very interesting, and extremely populous. Many chateaus appear in all directions, but none of them kept up in any style, and many of them falling into decay. Near the village of Merriville, I was lodged in a chateau of great magnificence, where it would require a very ample fortune to support in a manner suitable to its scale. It is the property of a widow, whose husband was seized in this mansion, during the phrensy of the revolution; and being a gentleman of wealth and power among the aristocrats, was dragged to the guillotine, where he forfeited his life to the rapacious desires of the predominant party. His widow, unable to continue the necessary splendor of the chateau, retired to Paris, to live upon her broken fortune; leaving a trusty domestic in charge of the house, and such furniture, and other valuables, as had escaped the cupidity of the revolutionists.

This magnificent chateau, is the finest I have seen in the country, and is well worthy of the notice of all travellers passing through these parts, as it probably furnishes one of the best specimens of the remains of feudal grandeur to be met with in France. The rooms, which are numerous throughout the building, and admirably arranged, are spacious, costly, and elegantly furnished, while comfort and convenience, appear to be every where united. The various paintings which are distributed about the principal rooms, form no mean collection. A set of Claude Lorrain's, in particular, arrested my attention as the finest I had ever seen.—The extensive grounds belonging to this delightful mansion are on a scale of beauty and magnificence commensurate with the edifice itself.

Though the country, from Orleans to the neighbourhood of the metropolis, is pleasing, from the variety and abundance of verdure and foliage, with which it abounds, yet it is less cultivated than farther south. Corn and grapes are grown in less quantities, and it contains a much greater proportion of waste land, and less inclosures. On our way hither, we passed through the small but handsome town of Rambouillet, where the celebrated hunting mansion of Buonaparte, bearing his name, is situated. The house is spacious, and elegantly built of white stone, and stands in a beautiful park, surrounded by fine woods. It was at this place that the Emperor first met the Arch-duchess, previously to his marriage. A magnificent suite of stables, called La Petite Ecurie, is attached to the premises.

I have noticed, I believe every thing, so far as my experience has gone, worthy of remark in this district, and shall again return to our progressive march. The latter stages of our route have been confined to places of secondary import only, such as Montfort, Mantes, and Estampes; which, however, are situated in the midst of very beautiful scenery, though they have nothing particular to recommend them, beyond what may be usually expected from small towns on the high road, in the neighbourhood of a metropolis.

I shall, therefore, conclude this letter, and defer till I have reached the coast, many general remarks which have occurred to me during my progress; in order that I may speak of the customs and manners of the nation at large, with more coolness and greater certainty than I am at present able to command.

Paris

Paris, July, 1814. Had I not been fully prepared to find the general aspect of Paris just what it is, I should certainly have felt disappointed upon a cursory view of it; as, in regard to its size, and the appearance of its streets, it is upon a very inferior scale to that which the imagination might naturally form, of the capital of so powerful and distinguished a nation as France. As I entered the city by the western barrier, when the setting sun, upon a beautiful summer's evening, shed a splendor over the surrounding scenery, and displayed the whole to the greatest possible advantage, my first impression of the city was extremely favourable; and my ideas of it were much raised, by the striking appearance of the Bois de Boulogne, and les Champs Elysees, having the chateau and gardens of the Thuilleries upon my right, and La Place Vendome upon my left; altogether certainly embracing the finest objects which this city can boast of, and fully calculated to afford the idea of a grand and magnificent metropolis. But, as I passed more into the interior of the place, I could not avoid being reminded pretty forcibly of Sterne's observations upon a similar occasion, and hoped with him, that the city might itself, upon a more extended acquaintance with it, "look better than it smelt," and wished that "the streets were but a thought wider." With respect to the generality of the streets, there are many to be found much more handsome in the best provincial towns; nor is this celebrated city, in this respect, equal to the exterior appearance, even of (he principal parts of Lisbon. It is also excelled, I am told, by Madrid, in the general *coup-d'œil*, and with London, it has not the smallest pretensions to vie. Notwithstanding these disadvantages, however, it has attractions to boast of in such infinite variety, as I believe, are scarcely to be rivalled in any other capital. In spite of the narrowness, and dirty state of the streets, and the almost entire deficiency of flagged pavement, it is impossible not to feel interest and delight in walking through them. To enter minutely into a detail of every novelty in this city, would require much more time than I can afford to devote for the purpose. I shall merely, therefore, attempt to give you the feelings and ideas with which some of the principal features have impressed me. For descriptions of Paris are so common, and every item has been so frequently described, that it would be an useless piece of tautology to dwell materially upon every thing which attracts and interests a stranger. The various curiosities, native as well as foreign, with which this city abounds, appear, upon inspecting the list, to be so multifarious and unusual, that I scarcely know how, during a residence of a few days, to reduce it to any sort of regular arrangement.

The Galleries of Pictures and Statues in the Louvre, unquestionably demand pre-eminence of attention before every other exhibition. To give you any thing like an adequate description of those magnificent specimens of art would require volumes, a large portion of time, and an acquaintance with the subject, which I do not affect to possess. I shall, therefore, content myself with endeavouring to present you with a very general view of those noble monuments of human genius.

The Gallery of Statues is divided into several "salles," or halls, each of which derives its name from its containing some principal figure or figures of antiquity,—thus, there is the Salle des Saisons—de L'Apollon— du Laocoon &c.—from those celebrated statues peculiarly ornamenting the respective divisions of the gallery in which they are placed. The effect produced by divisions, though it may partake somewhat of prettiness, is certainly deficient in grandeur; and in the imposing appearance, which might have been accomplished by a more skilful arrangement of the statues in one spacious hall or temple, classically designed and appropriately decorated, for the reception of the illustrious remains of former ages. In their present situation the general effect is poor and insipid, in comparison with that, which, I am told, they produced before French violence and rapacity had torn them from their magnificent and venerated abodes in the Italian States. Of the statues themselves, whether individually or collectively considered, it is impossible to speak in sufficiently high terms. I believe I may safely affirm, that there is not an indifferent piece of sculpture even throughout the collection; and some of the specimens are so exquisitely graceful, and inimitably correct and beautiful, that they equally defy the language of the author to describe, or the pencil of the artist to delineate them.

Those that chiefly attracted my attention were the Group of the Laocoon; the Meleager; the Mercury; the Crouching Venus; the Venus de Medicis; and above all, the Apollo Belvedere.

The first of these, though certainly a very wonderful production, did not, I must confess, whether from the lowness of its present situation, or my own want of taste, come quite up to the ideas which the uniform accounts of travellers had led me to entertain of it; though I might perhaps find it difficult to point out in what particular it disappointed me. The body and thighs of the Mercury (called also the Belvedere Antinous,) surpass almost every thing in the Gallery, for fleshiness of effect, and beauty of form; but the legs of the figure are too small, and the feet are supposed to have been supplied by some ancient Roman artist. The Crouching Venus is somewhat less than life, but is a beautiful little figure, and one of the most truly feminine characters I have ever seen. The front view of the Meleager is fine, but in others different parts of the body appear very inferior. The Venus de Medicis is the loveliest figure of woman I can imagine; but it strikes me to be merely a woman, and to partake very little of the character of the goddess. It has been much injured by time. To attempt a description of the astonishing statue of the Apollo, would, in me, be perfectly absurd. It strikes me as by far the greatest effort of human genius to be met with in this Gallery, or 1 should suppose in any other part of the world. Those who have seen casts only of this figure may form some conception of its beauties and general character, though their ideas must fall miserably short of that, with which a sight of the figure itself would furnish them. The youth, the majesty, the tremendous energy, and (if I may be allowed the expression,) downright motion of the figure, must be beheld first, before any just estimate can be formed of this inimitable work.

With this magical figure I shall conclude my remarks upon the Gallery of Statues, and proceed to that of the Pictures; the effect of which, even at the first entrance, is strikingly magnificent, and almost bewilders the sense.

The Gallery is divided into several compartments, some of which are of a immense extent, and one of them really looks, from its length and width, like another Pall-Mall. The whole of the walls are covered with the finest paintings, most of which form the most celebrated productions of the first masters of the art, and nearly all of the rest are greatly above mediocrity. They are divided into distinct classes, according to their respective schools, and much pains and considerable taste appear to have been shewn in their arrangement.

In speaking of the pictures (which I enter upon with great diffidence,) I shall confine myself merely to three or four, that struck me more particularly than the rest; though, there are so many possessing almost equal claims to excellence, that I hardly know whether I am doing them justice by making so partial a selection; but, what am I to do, surrounded as I am, by most of the best works of such artists as Raphael, Titian, Guido, Corregio, Poussin, Paul Veronese Rubens, Domenichino, &c. each of whose works it would require a volume to describe? As it is impossible then to mention all, I must content myself with giving you an account of a few of the most striking productions, such as the Transfiguration, by Raphael; the St. Peter, Martyr, by Titian; and the Deluge, by Nicolas Poussin.

The Transfiguration has been so often and so ably described, that I had little to add respecting it. It is certainly a very fine and uncommon picture, but I suspect that at first you would not greatly admire it. It is so very different in its appearance from any of the pictures we are accustomed to see in modern times, and is formed upon such very opposite principles, that it is some time before the eye can accustom itself to the sharp accuracy of its outlines, and scattered nature of its effect. After I had, however, attentively contemplated the picture, my eye became gradually reconciled to its peculiarities. Of all the pictures I have ever seen, the Transfiguration gives me the best idea of an assemblage of men in the open air; and nothing can exceed the drawing of the figures, the strength of the characters, the truth of the expressions, and the dignified propriety of the whole design. It is a picture to be studied deeply, and not merely seen.

The Murder of St. Peter, Martyr, seems to be the most perfect picture in the Gallery; for it unites in an eminent degree almost every excellence of the art. The landscape part is wild, savage, and lonely, admirably suited to the subject, and most powerfully executed; no sign of cultivation appears throughout the scene but every thing seems remote from the footstep's of civilized man. The landscape in itself, alone, is terrible; with the addition of the figures, it forms a scene of horror, which I should think it scarcely within the scope of painting to surpass. The hardy and unrelenting ferocity of the robber, the trembling fear, and convulsive agonies of the flying monk, and the calm and dignified resignation of the murdered saint, are master-pieces of expression, that, as far as I have seen, have never been equalled by any hand. The colouring and effect of the picture are also inimitable.

The Deluge, by Poussin, though a comparatively small picture, struck me (and I believe is generally considered) as one of the first in the collection. It has probably acquired its reputation more from the extraordinary medium diffused over the whole, than from any other of its admirable qualities. The heavens seem to descend in one continued deluge, which silently and gradually swallows up the world. There is nothing in the picture that gives the idea of a turbulent and transient storm; the whole seems to go forward with solemn and dreadful certainty; inevitable and universal destruction seems at hand. The various groups of distressed figures, incidentally introduced throughout the scene, are happily conceived; but the most surprising thing to me in the whole picture is, the bloated and saturated appearance which the artist has contrived to throw into every object throughout the painting.

I mention these three pictures particularly, because I received more pleasure in looking at them than from most of the others; many of which, however, if my limits would permit, I should have great pleasure in describing to you, particularly the magnificent paintings by Rubens, Paul Veronese, and Tintoret; many of whose best works are here collected. Some pictures also, by Le Brun, of Alexander's Battles, are well worthy of notice, and make a figure among the wonders in art by which they are surrounded, that I should not have previously expected.

With this slight sketch of the Galleries of Pictures and Statues I shall now conclude my letter, hoping that what I have written may serve to entertain you, and furnish you with some idea, however imperfect an one, of these stupendous and magnificent collections.

Paris II

Paris, July, 1814. Since I last wrote to you, I have been to court, according to the customary etiquette of British officers in Paris; where, as you may well suppose, a most gracious reception is insured. The attentions paid by the King, and the royal family in general, to our officers, is strongly marked; nor is the household at large deficient in this respect; not indeed, that their civilities are confined to the military, *un Anglois* is a sufficient passport every where in Paris. No insolent police officers arrest your approach to the interior of the palace when in an undress, nor powdered lacquies, and *les messieurs qui mangent le bœf* (as the French term our beef-eaters) await, as with us, the indispensible fee. The anti-rooms, and state chambers of the Tuilleries are spacious, and magnificently furnished, and adorned with beautiful portraits and other paintings.

The whole palace is, indeed, of the capital of a great nation, not only in its interior decorations, but also in its external form; the extent, magnificence, and elegance of which are not to be easily paralleled. The gardens of the chateau, tastily laid out, and ornamented with fine statues, inclosed within a cresent of handsome iron-railings, the top of each rail gilded, form, with the Elysian Fields, and La Place de Louis Quinze (*ci-devant* Place de la Revolution) a *coup-d'œil* unrivalled by any thing of the kind in our country. Within the chateau, on casting the eyes over the carved-work of the chambers, halls &c. as well as the stone-work without, monuments of Buonaparte's vanity are every where displayed, by the interposition of a large letter (N) between each medallion or compartment of the bass reliefs. This magical letter is, indeed, pretty liberally bestowed upon most public buildings throughout the city; nor has any opportunity been neglected, by this extraordinary man, to stamp a memento for posterity of his reign. In the pursuit of his ambitious projects, Paris has undoubtedly gained much advantage; and, it now wears, as I am assured by some who knew it before the revolution, a very imposing aspect, compared with its appearance in former days. Monuments and bridges, illustrative of his victories and fame, are perpetually to be met with; streets are widened, public buildings repaired and newly adorned, and several edifices erected while institutions have been formed, and old ones improved, very greatly for the public benefit.

Being driven about the town one day, in an hackney-coach, I stopped to observe some objects of curiosity, in an unfinished state, and among them the celebrated fountain of the elephant. My coachman, who possessed great acuteness, and much information, answered all my endless questions with the usual vivacity of the French; and told me, that this fountain was a thought of Buonaparte's, to employ the spare bronze, made from the cannon taken at Austerlitz, which remained after casing the column erected in La Place de Vendome to commemorate the deeds of the grand army. I asked him, when it was commenced, and when Louis XVIII would finish it. To the latter question he replied, with a significant shrug of the shoulders, and an indescribable and emphatic puckering up of his mouth into a look of perfect contempt—*"Jamais!"* making, at least, four syllables of the word, of which the finest actor could not have given the whole meaning, and the feelings, which accompanied its pronunciation, with fuller effect. His *jamais* seemed to "stretch out to the crack of doom." It is this part of Buonaparte's character; his attention to the greatness of his kingdom; his improvements and endowments; and his victories, the emblems of which, he omitted no opportunities of subjecting to the perpetual notice of the nation, that has gained him the hearts of Frenchmen; while his weaknesses and vices are obscured in the blaze of glory, which has ever surrounded his impetuous career. If any good befel, it was Buonaparte's; if evil—*la mal fortune* was in fault, the season, the stars, or any thing, in short, but their Grand Empereur.

Among the various exhibitions worthy of notice, one of the most interesting is Le Jardin des Plantes, where the naturalist may find abundant sources of amusement, in almost every branch of natural history.

The gardens are spacious and finely laid out; the one appropriated to botany is preserved in exact and excellent order. A variety of animals have plats of ground and dens allotted to them, while the most ferocious beasts are confined in cages. An elegant brick palace, with a spacious yard and a large pool of water attached to it, and every suitable accommodation, is erected for the residence of his serene highness, the elephant, who has hitherto lived in a less spacious and comfortable place. Several attempts have been recently made, to conduct his stupendous majesty from the old to the new palace; but, his attachment to the former is so strong, that it has baffled, hitherto, all efforts to remove him, and he obstinately refuses all notices to quit.

A menagerie of rare and beautiful birds, forms another very attractive department of this grand national establishment. Within doors, the inanimate treasures of nature are arranged in the most extensive and complete manner I ever witnessed.

The collection of fossils, minerals, petrefactions, coralines, shells &c. as well as insects, birds, reptiles, and animals of every class and species, preserved in all their native beauty and perfection, almost leads the stranger to suppose, that he has been transported to the garden of paradise.—Another building is dedicated to human and comparative anatomy; together with innumerable specimens of monsters, and various diseases incident to our frame. The comparative anatomy is the most-extensive I ever saw, and exceeds every thing of the kind to be met with in our country.—Where real specimens cannot be preserved, models in wax, accurately exemplify various phenomena of animalization.

The preparation which seems to excite most popular curiosity, is that of the stomach of a boy, containing a little child in its foetal state. A similar circumstance, in a boy more advanced in years, has, I learn, been lately discovered in London, and the preparation deposited in the Hunterian Collection of the College of Surgeons. To such subjects, however, as these, I perhaps attach more interest than you are likely to feel; I shall therefore proceed to treat of others of a more generally pleasing nature.

Among the public buildings, the Hospital of Invalids forms one of the most distinguished ornaments of Paris, and being surmounted with a gilded dome, makes a conspicuous figure in almost every view of the city. The different halls, passages, and apartments belonging to this charity, are spacious and handsomely constructed. The mess-room 'for the officers ,as well as the, one appropriated to the privates, are particularly worthy of notice. The former is furnished with beautiful paintings, of various descriptions. The chapel, however, exhibits the principal attraction, from the beauty of its structure, and its containing several monuments erected to the memory of departed heroes; those of Turenne and Vauban being the finest. Around the inside of the dome, hundreds of trophies, taken from the enemies of the nation, were lately suspended, which, on the approach of the allies, were all burnt. Buonaparte has caused his name to be venerated among the veterans of this establishment, by having added to their comforts and amusements an extensive library, in which the invalids are allowed to read during certain hours of the day. A spacious garden and pleasure-grounds are attached to the building, in which the pensioners enjoy some employ merit and much recreation.

From this place, I paid a visit to L'Ecole Militaire, now converted into a spacious barrack. Adjacent to it, is the Champ de Mars, where my attention was directed to the embankments raised during the enthusiasm of the revolution, for the people to assemble and swear allegiance to the various ephemeral governments of that disastrous period.

On my return, I had an opportunity of seeing the Palais Bourbon; and in La Place de Louis Quinze, the coachman stopped his horses to point out the spot where Louis XVI. was executed; which of course, from the recollection of past times and occurrences, could not fail of exciting in my mind a strong, though melancholy feeling of the instability of all human greatness.

To those who are not unwilling to quit for a moment the "warm precincts of the cheerful day," and descend among the remains and sombre chambers of the dead, the Catacombs will afford a subject of much curiosity. After gaining the depth of about sixty-feet, by a spiral flight of steps, you have to traverse a subterraneous gallery of considerable extent, from which there are many dangerous ramifications. The gallery is circuitous and narrow, and on its walls are inscribed tablets &c. commemorative of various persons and events. Hence you arrive at the deposit of bones, amounting, as it is said, to two million four hundred thousand skeletons; abundant space still remaining for future inhabitants. Compartments are regularly laid out for these mortal remains, which are arranged perpendicularly, with great system and care. Some parts of the gallery lie an hundred feet from the surface of the earth; and my conductor led me about a post league in extent, on which occasion, we all (for I formed one of a large party) carried a wax taper, the reflections from which produced a very singular effect. However amply we were gratified by this visit, every one seemed rejoiced at regaining the light and warmth of the sun, after the chilling dampness of so gloomy a place. These sacred repositories are supposed to be about seven hundred years old, and were discovered about one hundred years ago. They are said, with what foundation I know not, to have been formed by digging for stone, in order to assist in building Paris. They first became a receptacle for bones about forty years ago, in consequence of the burial-ground of the city being overfilled. The revolution, as you may well suppose, has contributed pretty largely to this collection, and the bodies of the victims to its ravages, thrown promiscuously into the Catacombs, are walled up. The last deposition was made in 1814. This mode of burial is conducted by night, and by means of carriages contructed for the purpose. Among the names of visitors to this place, I observed that of the Emperor of Austria. Buonaparte has never seen it. Five times the population of Paris, it is said, can be contained in these vaults. Engineers are appointed to make regular inspections, and report from time to time to the prefect of the city, under whose direction the establishment is kept.

The propensity inherent in our nature, to view the remains of places which have formerly been distinguished by remarkable events, induced me to visit the site on which the Bastile stood, retaining vestiges only of its former position and strength, and mouldered into a mass of ruins.

The costly and elegant bridge of Austerlitz, not far from this spot, excites much admiration. It is at once the lightest and handsomest fabric of the kind I ever saw.

In this neighbourhood I was shown a fountain, which, during, the disturbances of 1792, was made to spout forth wine for two days together, in order to assist in maddening the passions of the people.

La Musee des Monumens Francais, occupied a considerable share of my attention. Monsieur Le Noir, to whom the world is indebted for this interesting exhibition, collected together the contents of this Museum from the wreck of the Revolution, when the churches were ransacked, and many monuments either entirely torn to pieces, or partially mutilated, and arranged them systematically (by centuries,) in the convent of the Augustins. The barbarous spoliation these monuments were subjected to was certainly sufficient excuse for their removal from their original stations; although, could their safety have been secured, it would have been sacrilege to have displaced them. The interior of the convent and the gardens are entirely dedicated to them, and in the latter they are arranged in as classical and suitable a manner as circumstances would allow. Among these the simple tomb of Heloise and Abelard, actually containing the ashes of these faithful and unfortunate lovers, surrounded by cypresses, attracts the most general interest.

I must not omit mentioning the church of Notre Dame, which, however, disappointed me. The Spanish cathedrals, and some of those in our own country are so infinitely superior to it, that it failed to excite much interest. Had not my ideas been raised previously by many accounts of it, I should perhaps have admired it more. The Imperial regalia kept in this church are the most popular objects of curiosity, and the gold service for high mass is very superb. The crown of Charlemagne, and some others, the sceptre

&c, are all exhibited here, together with the splendid robes of the Emperor and Empress, made of crimson velvet, and edged with rich embroidery and ermine's skin, and studded with gold bees. A golden globe, said to contain the crown of thorns placed on our Saviour's head, and a piece of the cross, are also shewn.

In my next I must conclude my hasty remarks on Paris.

Paris III

Paris, July, 1814. I shall now touch upon one or two more matters, and then, from necessity, draw my remarks on Paris to a conclusion. Of all the manufactories which I have seen, I have been most struck with Gobelin's tapestry, the only one of the kind, I believe, in Europe. It is exceedingly interesting.—While I was there, they were copying Le Thyere's celebrated picture of the execution of Brutus's Sons; the original of which rivets every one's attention, on entering the gallery of paintings in the Louvre, from the admirable manner in which the story is told.

The Porcelain manufactory, on the road to Versailles, is an object of universal curiosity, specimens of which will, no doubt, soon become common in England.

The Palace of the Luxembourg, forms another object worthy of notice, not only from the very splendid and well known gallery of pictures by Rubens, which it contains, but also from several other circumstances of attraction. While I was in the building, I went to see the House of Peers, which is fitted up in the most elaborate and elegant style. I was, however, more struck with the House of Commons, which, though less splendid, wears an aspect of classic taste, unrivalled by any thing of the kind which I have ever seen. The external form of the latter building is superior also to that of the first.

Of the evening amusements, the choice lies principally among the theatres, the gardens of Tivoli, and a promenade round the Palais Royale; which, at night, is much thronged, while the brilliancy of the lights, proceeding from the different cafes, restaurateurs, shops &c. contrasted with the sombre shades of the trees, add much to the beauty, gaiety, and liveliness of the varied, bustling scene perpetually going forward. To describe the theatres of Paris would be endless, for they are almost innumerable; none of them rival ours in dimensions and decoration, though the ballet, as got up at the

French opera, is infinitely superior to any thing of the kind I have ever seen in our own. The corps de ballet is more numerous and far better conducted, and nothing can exceed their dancing, or the whole of the scenic representation.

The gardens of Tivoli are delightful, and I think, excel, in many respects those of Vauxhall, especially in the fire-works. My time will not permit me to give you a more extended account, of the various interesting matters contained in this city, and I must proceed to draw my letter to a conclusion; for were I to attempt naming even all that I have seen, or every thing worthy of notice, I should extend my correspondence to limits far too wide for our mutual convenience and desires. The short period I have been obliged to allow myself in this city, has only served to give me a wish, at some future period, of revisiting its numerous attractions, when more leisure may be afforded me. With the city of Paris itself, regarding only its streets and houses, I cannot say that I am much fascinated; but of all the places on the face of the globe, where a man, with time at his command, may best enjoy either a sensual or intellectual existence, Paris I should conceive, to be the most pre-eminent; for I know of no place, where every taste and pursuit can be more fully gratified with so little trouble and expense. The literati, the philosopher, the man of science, the naturalist, the artist, and even the man of pleasure, may here all find themes for consideration and amusement. There is, notwithstanding, one point of view in which Paris does not present so favourable an aspect; I allude to the state of society. This has experienced the effects of the revolution in a reversed ratio to that which has influenced the various sources of intellectual and sensual enjoyment above named. While the former have thrived, and, as it were, risen from the confusion of revolutionary times, the latter has decayed in a degree too sensible to escape the commonest observer.

Where refined and fashionable society, or even the more ordinary kind, exists in France, I am at a loss to know.—One would naturally be led to look for it in the metropolis, but there we should seek it in vain. Where, I have asked, are the people of fashion? where their equipages? their houses?—The reply has ever been, there are none to be found. Terror, dismay, confusion, and uncertainty have so long prevailed throughout all ranks of society; the dictatorial arm of military despotism has so long swayed the country; the cries of war have so long wrung in the ears of the nation, that some years of peace are requisite in order to re-establish that order of things, which, by banishing distrust and doubt, can alone restore the blessings of civil society, and mutual and friendly intercourse among the people. Under the benign and paternal influence of Louis's reign it is to be hoped, this desired state of society may be in due time restored, and united by firm bonds to those undeniable advantages which have grown out of the turbulence of past days.

But while I am thus indulging in speculations of the future, I forget for a moment that Buonaparte lives; that his marshals, who have profited by his ambitious career, also live, and that the army is disbanded, and, in a great measure, has lost its occupation, and its hopes; while the soldiery, on returning to domestic life, have little better to cheer themselves with, than the contemplation of all the evils which poverty and inoccupation induce.

I am as much disposed as you, or anyone equally loyal, can be, to flatter myself with the most sanguine expectations of the new government, and position of affairs in France. But, when I reflect upon the temper of the nation, and consider that the blow struck by all Europe in arms against it has fallen short of complete subjugation; I tremble for the consequences of a little breathing time to the people, and cannot induce myself to believe, without having that belief shaken by doubts, that the renewal of the "good old times" will be universally hailed with permanent cordiality throughout the country; mingled with the desired blessings of those times, there are circumstances, of which the altered state of public feeling, I am convinced, will never reconcile itself to the entire adoption.

Should a just and cautious respect be paid to both old and new systems, it is possible the Bourbons may prevail; but without attending to a proper medium, without leaning a little to reigning principles and prejudices, I, for my part, entertain little hopes of lasting peace, and unthreatened dominion to the restored family upon the throne.

Towards the Sea

Cantonments, near Boulogne, July, 1814. After having fully gratified, in the manner I have described, my ardent desire of visiting Paris, and which the delays attendant upon embarkation afforded me sufficient opportunity of indulging, I posted the remainder of my journey to the coast about Boulogne. I shall now proceed to conclude the long and highly interesting tour, which I have had the good fortune to accomplish, from a point which a few months back the most sanguine expectation could scarcely have predicted we should ever have arrived at.

In journeying from Paris we have fallen in with so many of our countrymen, that I have from that period scarcely been able to consider myself in foreign country. All things appear to wear the stamp of British habits and manners, the English are every where talked of, and their language is commonly understood. The most common enquiry made by my countrymen has been chiefly with respect to the reception we experienced in our passage through France. You will bear in mind that in our march through the country on our return to England, when the object of the British army entering France was accomplished, and the fate of the country decided, that the feelings of the people must have been greatly altered in consequence of the late decided turn which affairs have subsequently taken. Any one imagining that we could be received universally with open arms, and greeted with general enthusiasm and heartfelt satisfaction, must, under the existing circumstances of the case, be very ignorant indeed of the feelings that commonly actuate human nature, and with those which lead this nation in particular, for, its predominant character being that of vanity, little indulgence can be expected by those who have so materially contributed to mortify their feelings, and humble their national pride.

The French appear to me warm and sanguine while any great events are pending, and this disposition they all individually evince to whatever side they may incline. But throughout the whole race one paramount idea absorbs every other—a devotedness to the interests of their own country, and an utter abhorrence from the interference of every other in their internal government. They may, like ourselves, be dissatisfied with this or that ruling party in the state, but, if a moment should be left them for reflection, they would rise one and all to repel the attempts of a foreign invader, and no sacrifice would be considered too great to preserve the integrity of the country.

Two circumstances weigh very powerfully in impressing Englishmen with an idea of their not being well received by a nation which has so long shown itself a determined and gallant enemy. In the actual situation of the two countries how is it possible to expect any thing very different from what has really occurred? The French, in the first instance, from the unexpected change of affairs, have been severely mortified by the prowess of that country, which, in the pride of victory, they had affected to despise; and, in the second place, something of a similar nature must have occurred from the consciousness that their present situation, instead of proceeding from themselves, has been forced upon them by the strong arm and united powers of those nations upon which they had so recently trampled.

It may be naturally conceived that these two circumstances combined, tended to produce an irritable feeling and dissatisfaction, which the very march of British troops through the heart of their country had a disposition to augment.

With some exceptions, the inhabitants of the southern provinces appear to be more generally in favour of the restoration of the Bourbons than those bordering upon the metropolis, and to manifest a warmer friendship for the British. But, wherever any of the French troops are found, it may easily be supposed the natural rivalry and jealousy existing between the two nations is ready to burst forth. Nevertheless, I am inclined to believe, that instances of open insult to the military are of much less frequent occurrence than is generally supposed; though certainly some instances of the kind have taken place. In the town of Montauban the following outrage occurred, which, as it happened under my own knowledge, I shall here relate. A British officer, who, in compliment to the new order of things, had mounted the white cockade, was attacked by a party of French officers in the interest of Buonaparte, who endeavoured, in a rude and forcible manner, to tear it from his cap. The English officer of course resisted this violent and unjustifiable outrage, and an old French officer arriving at the moment, and taking an active part in the business, put an end to the affray, reprobated the conduct of his brother officers, and declared the English officer to have acted with the most perfect propriety, and the upshot of the whole was that a fair challenge from the latter, in consequence of the insult he received, was refused in the most evasive and dastardly manner.

Our intercourse being very slender with the higher ranks of society, and our connection, from the circumstances of their situation, with the lower orders, very limited, it is, perhaps, not very surprising that the latter should have endeavoured to make the most of us during our passage through the country. And, I must acknowledge, that they were not in general behind hand in practising every species of extortion, which, it is perhaps only justice to admit, that the French themselves would inevitably have experienced had they been travelling through our own country in a similar manner. That there was an uniform, or even frequent disposition to annoy and insult the

English, I have no hesitation in denying most positively; and so far as my experience has gone, the French in general have behaved with more hospitality, civility and kindness, than the Spaniards, who were bound by the strongest ties of moral obligation to acknowledge by every means in their power the eminent services we had rendered them, services which can admit of no question, desired by themselves, necessary to their welfare, and without which they must actually have failed of finally accomplishing their purposes. However much we, who stand aloof from the prejudices of the French, must dislike the policy of their late usurper, and regard with somewhat of self-complacency the recent change of affairs, which has been brought about chiefly by our own exertions, yet we must not allow prejudice so far to blind us, as to make it a cause for wonder and astonishment, that the feelings of the French nation are not altogether in unison with our own. But, as this is a subject which might carry me to greater lengths than I can at present afford time to devote to it, I content myself with giving you merely a general idea of our reception during our passage through the country. In doing this I have perhaps succeeded in shewing you that the respect and admiration almost universally entertained for the abilities of Buonaparte, cannot easily be eradicated; and no thing, I am convinced, will reconcile the people at large to the late peace, the very nature of which, by circumscribing their possessions, and in some respects lowering their national character, can scarcely be expected to be very popular among them. It remains to be ascertained whether the coercion which has been necessarily used by the Allies, will be likely to produce those disinterested ends, which I am willing to suppose first led to the late formidable coalition against the unjust pretensions of this powerful and dangerous nation.

With respect to the state of religion in this country, or rather to the almost absolute want of it, it is very difficult to speak either with accuracy or impartiality. The great indifference to subjects of this nature observable, among the larger proportion of the people, and the extreme bigotry of the remainder to all their former superstitious notions, are I fear very likely to open a wide door of the re-establishment of the Catholic religion with all its powers and abuses. I am induced to say this, not only from the instances which I have myself witnessed of the returning tide of prejudice and superstition, but also from the natural tendency of human nature, ever prone to proceed from the excess of licentiousness to the most violent intolerance, and vice versa.

During the performances of high mass, I have observed a striking mixture of those two most distinct feelings, though the latter is at this moment evidently gaining ground. The activity of the catholic priests in promoting prosylitism is almost proverbial, and when aided, as it now is by the military arm, cannot fail of making in a short time, the most rapid progress. The circumstances which I have often witnessed during divine service, in several places, will, perhaps, better elucidate the few reflections I have ventured to make, than by giving any further detail of my opinions upon the subject.

In one church, where curiosity had induced me and some others to be present, while divine service was performing, we were desired by one of the gens-d'armes in attendance, to leave the church, unless we openly conform to all the discipline of Catholicism, and we accordingly felt ourselves under the necessity of withdrawing.

From the specimens I had seen in Portugal and Spain, and the many instances I had heard of the contempt shown for all sacred institutions by the French armies, I was not a little surprized at this extraordinary display of sanctity, which I believe, would scarcely have been tolerated in the most bigoted times of old France. The inhabitants, upon the occasion of this ceremony, which had commenced in the church, and was afterwards continued through the principal streets of the town, by special order, hung their walls with white sheets, and raised several altars, decorated with garlands of flowers, and various other ornaments in the midst of them. The procession moved from the church, accompanied by a number of priests and other customary attendants, and the host was carried under an elegant canopy, while a lamb decorated with blue ribbons, was led to one of the altars, and then sacrificed. The whole was performed with great stage effect, and protected by a large party of the gens-d'armes, who enforced the strictest obedience and respect from every bystander, prohibiting at the same time the approach of every Englishman, unless he presented himself uncovered. And as they were pretty summary in their proceedings, several officers, either from ignorance or inattention, experienced very gross insults; which however, upon a representation to the proper authorities were highly disapproved of, though the instances having occurred tend to shew pretty clearly the altered temper and disposition of the people. I was informed that it was a common belief among many of the people and very frequently expressed, that we had no religion at all; to which I replied, that it was our custom to perform our devotions more in private, without the aid of military parade, or the gorgeous processions and imposing ceremonies of the catholic church, though probably that our ideas respecting religious subjects were not less sincere than their own. As to the priests, we are, I believe, universally esteemed by them as obstinate heretics; and, indeed, one of the former, speaking of our brigade, which he much admired, added, that it was very lamentable to see so many fine fellows who had no chance of salvation.

With these remarks I shall now conclude my letter, and may probably, in case of farther detention, find some subjects of amusement yet untouched upon that may furnish matter for a concluding letter.

Epilogue

Cantonments, near Boulogne, July, 1814. As it has turned out, according to my expectations, that our embarkation is still delayed, I am enabled to furnish you with the few remaining observations alluded to in my last letter. The first subject, to which I shall direct your attention, will relate to the accommodations for travelling afforded in France, when compared with those of Portugal and Spain. With England it is useless to make a comparison, as we all well know the general superiority of our own country over that of every other, in the facility and comforts open to travellers of every description. The chief distinction observable between travelling in France and the adjacent countries beyond the Pyrenees, consists in the opportunity every where afforded in the former of procuring carriages of all kinds, together with the abundant distribution of hotels, inns, restaurateurs &c, whereas in Portugal and Spain, the former particularly, there being very few roads capable of affording a passage to wheeled-carriages beyond a short distance, the only choice left for the traveller is to adopt the usual practice of those countries, of riding upon mules, which, for numerous and obvious reasons, is subject to a variety of inconveniencies; to this may be added, not only the great distances you may have to travel before any posada or inn presents itself, but also the frequent deficiency of comfortable accommodation at such places, and the scarcity and bad quality of the food. In these essential points, France, as in every other point of civilization, greatly exceeds both her western neighbours.

And moreover, a traveller in this country is not exposed, as he perpetually is in the others, to plunder, robbery, and assassination atrocities, which the slow pace of the post mules, and the exposure of the persons of their riders, very greatly contributes to promote. The inns or auberges in France certainly exceeded greatly the ideas I had previously formed of them.—Though many exceptions to the contrary are sometimes met with, yet I generally found them much less inferior to our own than I had been led to believe, and have not unfrequently been quartered in some hotels &c. which are spacious, elegant, and even (what your national prejudice will perhaps scarcely allow you to credit) very cleanly; the landlords of which, are as civil and attentive, and furnish, I assure you, as good and wholesome meals, as you will meet with at the very best houses on the English roads. The older inns are undoubtedly totally out of the pale of this favourable account, but in respect to many of the modern auberges it is strictly true. One of the principal luxuries which I have enjoyed in the latter, is the excellence of their beds, the construction and arrangement of which are to my mind even preferable to the common method adopted in England. On the high road to Paris, from the coast about Boulogne &c. you would not find my assertions at all verified; but, were you to pass to the southward, I am convinced you would subscribe to the justness of these remarks. The signs of the different *auberges* resemble ours, as *lion d'or, lion argent, grand cerf, soleil d'or, l'aigle d'or* &c.

At almost all of these places the eye is attracted by the words *bon double bierre*, often written upon a sheet of coloured paper, accompanied with a drawing, which represents a gentleman and lady equipped in travelling dresses, supposed to be refreshing themselves on the way, with this favourite beverage; and in order to indicate its peculiar excellence, the happy pair are seen (according to our English phrase of hobbing and nobbing) to bring their glasses into contact, while the effervescent contents foam from one into the other. In many instances I have found this liquor deserving of its reputation, and usually far preferable to the generality of their *bon vin* the latter of which is often extremely weak and acidulous, somewhat indeed resembling in quality a mixture of cyder and vinegar. Superior wine is however to be met with, though I do not think that the *vin du paye ordinaire* of France is to be compared with the country wines of Portugal and Spain.

The great profusion of these auberges caused billets to be issued by the magistrates repeatedly upon them, during our march through the country; so that instead of being quartered, as in Portugal and Spain, upon private families, our abode was more frequently in public-houses, much to the advantage of the inn-keepers, though seldom to that of ourselves. Besides the auberges in large towns there are man *chambres à louer*, announced on the outside of large houses, the various inhabitants of which are usually not of the most select description, and, from the construction of the rooms, privacy and comfort are out of the question. I was once quartered on such a place, and on enquiring for my room, was introduced to a spacious dirty garret, furnished with several broken-down bedsteads, chairs, and tables, adorned with old and dirty moth-eaten green tapestry, altogether presenting so woeful an appearance as could scarcely have been paralleled in Grub-street.

There being no less than four different doors communicating with various lesser rooms and passages, it was late before the numerous lodgers ceased to pass and repass, and when I deemed it prudent, I followed the example of those who occupied the other beds (among which was an whole family of children in one) and prepared to stretch myself on my dirty couch.

Before however I could effect this completely, a party, consisting of an old man and three women, (all intoxicated) accompanied by two children, burst into the room, apparently arrived from some fair or revel, and seated themselves with perfect sang-froid round a table, to enjoy their supper before they retired to rest. In vain I remonstrated, and insisted upon my right to the privacy of the room, in order to get to bed. *"Restez tranquile, monsieur,"* was the only answer I could obtain, and it was not without considerable opposition and difficulty, on my part, that I at length persuaded them to retire to their chamber, where they all went to sup and to sleep. Early the next morning I was awakened by my busy fellow-lodgers, and without much stretch of imagination, might easily have conceived myself to be lying in an open street, in the most frequented part of the town, from the multiplicity of people that continually passed and repassed by the foot of my bed, leaving me in as little hopes of avoiding rising, as I had experienced of sleeping, in public. This chamber seemed to be the focus where all the lodgers concentrated. At one end I saw, on looking through my curtain, a party at breakfast, by the side of the fire some children were having their feet washed, and the ladies *en papilotte et dishabile*, were preparing for the recreations of a Sunday morning, while a group was in constant motion before me, among which I noticed filles, garcons, shoe-brushers, old-clothesmen, (one of whom actually enquired of me as I lay in bed, if I had any small clothes, or other garments for sale) with an host of people of all kinds, making my corner of the room a perfect thoroughfare. You may readily conceive, that my first care on getting up, was to apply for another billet, which Monsieur Maire, with many condolences for my bad lodging, very readily afforded me.

With reference to the facility of conveyance from place to place, it may not be unamusing to you, perhaps, were I to endeavour to describe the manner in which the most common vehicles are conducted.

To any one acquainted with Sterne's excellent description of the French people and manners, it may appear superfluous to enter into a detail of matters already so well described; but there are some circumstances which, however accurately pourtrayed, fall so very far short of reality, that I cannot help noticing them. The liveliest imagination among the charicaturists of our own country, have never yet approached the grotesque reality of a French postillion, it is in short a non-descript animal, which few naturalists have ventured to delineate, and their prudence is truly commendable, upon a subject where eloquence itself must fail.

In however ludicrous a light the French postillions may appear, they certainly meet with an equal parallel in the extraordinary vehicles which in this country are used for the same purposes of our stage coaches. The great public *diligence*, which, from its name, reminds me of the reason given for a grove being termed in Latin *lucus*, i.e. *a non lucendo*, is really a curiosity in all its points. Its weight, from the quantity of thick iron and wood work, is immense, and its motion proportionably slow, usually requiring nearly a dozen horses to move it with an activity somewhat resembling the speed of our stage waggons, the animals being marshalled in so extraordinary a manner as completely to confound all calculations of utility and arrangement excepting such as reside in the imagination of a French postillion. I have myself witnessed a team of this description (if I may be allowed the expression) placed in the following singular style. Two horses placed abreast in the limbers, (carrying by-the-bye the whole weight of the carriage) were succeeded by three on one side, and two on the other, placed about halfway, but not quite equidistant from the hinder ones, and three others were placed irregularly before them, forming altogether a species of pyramid, which, as it may be very naturally supposed, completely despised taking any share in forwarding the progression and advance of the carriage, the principle labour of which fell upon the ill-star'd animals behind.—Under the circumstances, necessary to the conducting of this complicated affair, I leave it to you as matter for speculation, to conjecture in what place the driver of this motley group chose to take up his position? Perhaps you would naturally suppose that he would post himself behind the two limber horses, or possibly be mounted upon the leader; no such thing—he very quietly seated himself upon the near horse of that row immediately succeeding the two shaft horses, and with an intrepidity very worthy of admiration, directed the whole with a persuasive and truly national crack of the whip with as much *sang-froid* and management as one of our own postillions would conduct a single pair of horses.

I shall now speak of the various asylums, hospitals &c. which do great credit to the nation, and embrace every species of helpless objects. I have seen no place so small but it possesses some plan of protection for the sick and lame; the attention of the females in particular being highly exemplary, and in the absence of that excellent and social order, Les Sœurs de la Charité', ladies of all classes are in the habit of performing the offices of matrons in rotation to the different hospitals. Among these establishments, the most interesting appeared to me to be those *pour les Enfans abandonnés*, and the asylums for the deaf and dumb. The former are arranged into different classes according to the years of the children and other circumstances. One room is appropriated indiscriminately to infants of both sexes; a second to girls of a more advanced age; and a third to the elder boys, the whole presenting a sight really gratifying, as happiness, content, cheerfulness and industry seem to reign throughout the whole of these establishments. It may readily be supposed that such advantages are eagerly sought after in a nation so reduced and impoverished as France, by parents, who, though possessing the will, may be deficient in the means of maintaining their offspring.

In Bourdeaux there were 2800 children put out to nurse at one time, by a single institution alone, while 400 were maintained within doors, together with 60 infants newly born, by the same charity.

The mode of receiving children into these asylums may appear to you somewhat singular, a frame-work poised upon a swivel is placed at the outer door, in which the little foundling is laid, and this being turned round, presents the forsaken orphan to the notice of those whose business it is to take it in, where it cannot long remain unobserved, as its screams, acting in concert with the sound of a bell connected with the above machinery, quickly brings it assistance. During the reign of Napoleon, these institutions proved a fruitful nursery for the army; and as these establishments perhaps contributed in no small degree to the fartherance of his favourite system of policy, they most probably (while the country was under his sway) met with all due encouragement.

The asylums for the deaf and dumb are all constructed upon the ingenious principle of the Abbé de La Pée, and his successor, the Abbé Sicard. I have always observed more intelligence marked in the features of his pupils than in the generality of those who are in the full possession of all their faculties.

Yet notwithstanding the many charitable institutions which this nation affords, perhaps none exceeds France in the multiplicity and importunity of its beggars. In the southern provinces the traveller is less infested with them than in the northern, and especially in the environs of the metropolis, and on the road between Paris and Calais, where they swarm to a degree which is almost inconceivable. It is no uncommon thing for an whole village apparently to sally forth when strangers are approaching, while petitions from every mouth—*"Pour l'amour du Dieu,"* addressed most pathetically to *"Mi Lord Anglois,"* and assail the hapless travellers, whose carriage they one and all surround in the most importunate manner. In spite however of the apparent distress which is to be discovered in every individual that applies to you, it is curious to observe, that notwithstanding the unfortunate circumstances in which the people of the country have for a long time been placed, the natural politeness of the French is still in a degree predominant over every other feeling. It is no uncommon thing to see persons in the predicament I have mentioned, whose appearance bears evident marks of the most abject poverty, giving place to females, not perhaps in worse circumstances than themselves, and, in Sterne's language, crying out "place aux dames." I have witnessed scenes of this kind more than once; and in one instance in particular I recollect, when the carriage was surrounded by a number of these mendicants, that an old woman, who had apparently been long bed-ridden, was brought down with some difficulty upon two men's shoulders and, though the carriage at the time was pretty thickly surrounded, every other claimant instantly gave way, and a lane was made by common consent for a passage to the vehicle, every man upon this occasion (as was pretty audibly expressed,) instantly resigning his own pretensions in favour of those of the other sex.

With these remarks I shall now conclude my correspondence, and those reflections which have resulted from my march through the three kingdoms; which, from the recent and indeed present posture of affairs, may perhaps be considered as among the most interesting states of modern Europe.

In the course of my progress I have endeavoured to touch upon those subjects which my scanty means of obtaining information have afforded, taking it for granted that nothing relating to Portugal, Spain, and France, agitated and convulsed as they have been during late years, can prove altogether devoid of interest and amusement. However much my endeavours may fall short of the subject, you will not, I trust, accuse me of vanity when I assume that merit at least which arises from having studiously avoided setting down any thing with partiality, or which my own experience did not teach me to rely upon as absolutely authentic.

ALSO FROM LEONAUR

AVAILABLE IN SOFTCOVER OR HARDCOVER WITH DUST JACKET

WELLINGTON AND THE PYRENEES CAMPAIGN VOLUME I: FROM VITORIA TO THE BIDASSOA *by F. C. Beatson*—The final phase of the campaign in the Iberian Peninsula.

WELLINGTON AND THE INVASION OF FRANCE VOLUME II: THE BIDASSOA TO THE BATTLE OF THE NIVELLE *by F. C. Beatson*—The second of Beatson's series on the fall of Revolutionary France published by Leonaur, the reader is once again taken into the centre of Wellington's strategic and tactical genius.

WELLINGTON AND THE FALL OF FRANCE VOLUME III: THE GAVES AND THE BATTLE OF ORTHEZ by *F. C. Beatson*—This final chapter of F. C. Beatson's brilliant trilogy shows the 'captain of the age' at his most inspired and makes all three books essential additions to any Peninsular War library.

NAVAL BATTLES OF THE NAPOLEONIC WARS *by W. H. Fitchett*—Cape St. Vincent, the Nile, Cadiz, Copenhagen, Trafalgar & Others

SERGEANT GUILLEMARD: THE MAN WHO SHOT NELSON? *by Robert Guillemard*—A Soldier of the Infantry of the French Army of Napoleon on Campaign Throughout Europe

WITH THE GUARDS ACROSS THE PYRENEES by *Robert Batty*—The Experiences of a British Officer of Wellington's Army During the Battles for the Fall of Napoleonic France, 1813.

A STAFF OFFICER IN THE PENINSULA *by E. W. Buckham*—An Officer of the British Staff Corps Cavalry During the Peninsula Campaign of the Napoleonic Wars

THE LEIPZIG CAMPAIGN: 1813—NAPOLEON AND THE "BATTLE OF THE NATIONS" *by F. N. Maude*—Colonel Maude's analysis of Napoleon's campaign of 1813.

BUGEAUD: A PACK WITH A BATON by *Thomas Robert Bugeaud*—The Early Campaigns of a Soldier of Napoleon's Army Who Would Become a Marshal of France.

TWO LEONAUR ORIGINALS

SERGEANT NICOL by *Daniel Nicol*—The Experiences of a Gordon Highlander During the Napoleonic Wars in Egypt, the Peninsula and France.

WATERLOO RECOLLECTIONS by *Frederick Llewellyn*—Rare First Hand Accounts, Letters, Reports and Retellings from the Campaign of 1815.

ALSO FROM LEONAUR

AVAILABLE IN SOFTCOVER OR HARDCOVER WITH DUST JACKET

CAPTAIN OF THE 95th (Rifles) *by Jonathan Leach*—An officer of Wellington's Sharpshooters during the Peninsular, South of France and Waterloo Campaigns of the Napoleonic Wars.

BUGLER AND OFFICER OF THE RIFLES *by William Green & Harry Smith* With the 95th (Rifles) during the Peninsular & Waterloo Campaigns of the Napoleonic Wars

BAYONETS, BUGLES AND BONNETS by *James 'Thomas' Todd*—Experiences of hard soldiering with the 71st Foot - the Highland Light Infantry - through many battles of the Napoleonic wars including the Peninsular & Waterloo Campaigns

THE ADVENTURES OF A LIGHT DRAGOON *by George Farmer & G.R. Gleig*—A cavalryman during the Peninsular & Waterloo Campaigns, in captivity & at the siege of Bhurtpore, India

THE COMPLEAT RIFLEMAN HARRIS *by Benjamin Harris as told to & transcribed by Captain Henry Curling*—The adventures of a soldier of the 95th (Rifles) during the Peninsular Campaign of the Napoleonic Wars

WITH WELLINGTON'S LIGHT CAVALRY *by William Tomkinson*—The Experiences of an officer of the 16th Light Dragoons in the Peninsular and Waterloo campaigns of the Napoleonic Wars.

SURTEES OF THE RIFLES by *William Surtees*—A Soldier of the 95th (Rifles) in the Peninsular campaign of the Napoleonic Wars.

ENSIGN BELL IN THE PENINSULAR WAR *by George Bell*—The Experiences of a young British Soldier of the 34th Regiment 'The Cumberland Gentlemen' in the Napoleonic wars.

WITH THE LIGHT DIVISION by *John H. Cooke*—The Experiences of an Officer of the 43rd Light Infantry in the Peninsula and South of France During the Napoleonic Wars

NAPOLEON'S IMPERIAL GUARD: FROM MARENGO TO WATERLOO by *J. T. Headley*—This is the story of Napoleon's Imperial Guard from the bearskin caps of the grenadiers to the flamboyance of their mounted chasseurs, their principal characters and the men who commanded them.

BATTLES & SIEGES OF THE PENINSULAR WAR by *W. H. Fitchett*—Corunna, Busaco, Albuera, Ciudad Rodrigo, Badajos, Salamanca, San Sebastian & Others

AVAILABLE ONLINE AT
www.leonaur.com
AND OTHER GOOD BOOK STORES

NAP-1

www.ingramcontent.com/pod-product-compliance
Lightning Source LLC
LaVergne TN
LVHW091641100826
845152LV00006B/116/J

* 9 7 8 1 8 4 6 7 7 3 9 2 1 *